Pocket Guide to England

by

Evangeline Holland

Copyright © 2012-13 by Evangeline Holland

All rights reserved. No part of this publication may be reproduced, distributed, or transmitted in any form or by any means, including photocopying, recording, or other electronic or mechanical methods, without the prior written permission of the publisher, except in the case of brief quotations embodied in critical reviews and certain other noncommercial uses permitted by copyright law.

Chapter 1 : Introduction to the Edwardian Era 4

Chapter 2: Class in Edwardian England 9

Chapter 3: The Social Round 19

Chapter 4: London, A Sprawling Metropolis 28

Chapter 5: The Countryside 47

Chapter 6: Amusements and Entertainments 54

Chapter 7: Behind Closed Doors 62

Chapter 8: Edwardians Eat 81

Chapter 9: Social Transformations 97

Chapter 10: The Winds of Change 108

RESOURCES 131

ABOUT THE AUTHOR 136

Chapter 1: Introduction to the Edwardian Era

The Edwardian Era in its strictest form lasted from 1901 to 1910, during which Edward VII (1841-1910) reigned as King of the United Kingdom of Great Britain and Ireland and of the British Dominions and Emperor of India. However, in its broader interpretation, the spirit of the Edwardians—which was indelibly inspired by Edward VII during his tenure as Prince of Wales—stretched from 1880-1914. To further extend the cultural interpretation, I sometimes round up to 1924 because I consider the fall of Lloyd George, the steep decline of the Liberal Party, and the rise of Labour, to be the final break between society as the Edwardians knew it and Modern Britain.

In the Western World, the Edwardian era was a time of great social change and of a solidification of the power of the ruling elite. The French, with their eloquent and perceptive turns of phrasing, characterized the years between 1880 and 1914 as *La Belle Epoque* (the beautiful epoch) and *Fin de siècle* (a period of degeneration and of hope for a new beginning). Certainly no other time in history has witnessed such decadence and pessimism aligned with such optimism and hope.

Nevertheless, the Edwardians marched into the twentieth century with more optimism and hope than pessimism. Wealth was abundant and nearly tax free, Society was no longer the small, exclusive circle confined to the aristocracy, travel was cheap and easy (no passports or visas required, save at the Russian and Ottoman borders, and the Gold Sovereign was taken everywhere), and advances in flight, science, and industry made everyone confident that improved technology would bring peace.

More importantly, Great Britain was the most powerful nation in the world. The maxim coined for the Spanish Empire of the sixteenth and seventeenth centuries now rang true for the British Empire, and from London to Cape Town to Bombay to Vancouver and back again, the sun never set on the Union Jack, which waved with both vigor and sublime assurance. Granted, British might was tested by the small colonial skirmishes throughout the nineteenth century, but Jolly Old England was still "Home" to millions of subjects of various creeds, colors, religions, and class.

The Concert of Europe
Britain held itself mostly aloof from its European neighbors, but the deep, abiding family ties forged by the marriage of Queen Victoria's children into powerful European monarchies made that aloofness difficult, particularly when the British Royal Family were forced to choose sides. A particular *bête noir* was the German Empire, whose unification in 1871 in the wake of their defeat of France in the Franco-Prussian War exacerbated the tensions between the World Powers.

Prussia, the largest and most militarist German state, had been steered to greatness by Otto von Bismarck. Bismarck, a Junker (landed gentry) military leader and statesman, used the might of the Prussian army to shake up the balance of power established during the Congress of Vienna (1815) and then used his strong persuasive tactics to establish a new balance of power that tipped heavily in unified Germany's favor. From 1870 to 1890, when he fell out with the new Kaiser—Wilhelm II, Queen Victoria's grandson—Bismarck's checkmates across Europe resulted in the unification of Italy, the decline of the Ottoman Empire after the Russo-Turkish War (1877-78), and a series of alliances, double-crosses, and re-alliances that bore fruit in the chaos of war declarations in the summer of 1914.

Bismarck also extended a hand to a weakened but still massive Austria-Hungary, whose desire to expand its influence in the

Balkans butted against Russia's desire to protect its own interest amongst her fellow Slavs.

Britain eyed all of these shenanigans with a benevolent eye. She was more concerned with Empire building—and her own internal dramas, which ranged from a severe agricultural depression that lasted from the 1880s to Edward VII's ascension, to a demand in the increase in male enfranchisement, to the perennial question of Irish Home Rule. Eventually they could *not* cast a benevolent eye on Kaiser Wilhelm II, who could not resist bombastic, ambitious, saber rattling whenever he felt slighted or left out of international affairs.

A Place in the Sun
The Edwardian era was also the Imperial Age, and the Congress of Berlin (1878) and the Berlin Conference (1884) brought together the heads of state for every nation but the ones being carved up and parceled out as spoils! The former was called after the aforementioned Russo-Turkish War, and the unrest encouraged in the Balkans by the Great Powers. The Powers also supported the creation of Roumania, Serbia, and Bulgaria, hoping to swoop down on the remains of the Ottoman Empire. The latter was called to regulate the conquest of Africa when explorers and so-called benevolent missionaries discovered vast quantities of precious metals and other valuable resources, which sparked an aggressive "Scramble for Africa."

Bismarck held both conferences in his iron fist, but was eager to reassure Britain that both powerful nations could exist in harmonious fashion. Indeed, during this time the relationship between Great Britain and the German Empire was warm and cordial—the fruitfulness of Victoria and Albert's greatest wish to create a rapport between the two nations by marrying the Princess Royal to the Prussian Crown Prince (later Frederick III). Britain also worried little over the military prowess of the German Empire—their prowess lay in the navy, whose reputation remained unchallenged and undisputed. In fact, they continued to view France, their traditional enemy, with suspicion well into the early 1900s, and were never on easy terms with Russia, whom they felt had designs on India.

However, as events later proved, Britain's confidence (or arrogance, to be more precise) blinded them to the Kaiser's desire for a "place in the sun." Queen Victoria's grandson ascended to the throne in 1888 after the ninety-nine day reign of his father Frederick III, who succumbed to the inoperable throat cancer that was diagnosed before he even came to the throne. Characterized by his mother Vicky as "thoroughly Prussian," Wilhelm—known as Willy to his family—set about undermining Bismarck's iron grip on the running of the German Empire, and finally dismissed the Chancellor in 1890, after which he opted on a more personal rule. And that personal rule involved making Germany the dominant partner in Anglo-German relations.

Life in Britain
When Edward ascended the throne in 1901, the population of London was 4,536,641 in an area of just 118 square miles. According to Baedeker's *London*, "there are in London more Scotsmen than in Aberdeen, more Irish than in Dublin, more Jews than in Palestine, and more Roman Catholics than in Rome." The population of Great Britain and Ireland stood at 41,609,091, and a great majority now lived in cities, thus mirroring the agricultural decline of the late 19th century. Surprisingly, this agricultural depression did not shake Britain's confidence, though it did worry the farmers whose livelihood was jeopardized by the cheaper produce imported into the country from Germany, the Colonies, and America.

What *did* shake Britain's confidence?

The Second Boer War, a colonial skirmish between the British Army and the Boers (Dutch-speaking settlers), who did accept British rule, but did not accept the annexing of their republics (Free Orange State and the Transvaal) into the British Empire. The British marched into war expecting a quick victory against the rebellious Boers, but were soundly licked and turned into a laughing stock overnight. By the time the war limped to its embarrassing end, Britain's period of "splendid isolation" was over, and they were determined to find allies.

British politics also undermined the nation's confidence. The House of Commons was considered another "gentleman's club," and for most of the nineteenth century only gentlemen could afford to stand for Parliament—and only gentlemen possessed the franchise. Matters changed by the 1870s and 1880s when Prime Ministers Gladstone and Disraeli helped transform the Whigs and Peelites to the Liberal Party and the Tories to the Conservative Party, respectively.

The almost flip-flopping of governments between them from the 1860s until Disraeli's death in 1881 saw Britain steered through the increasing franchise of male voters, social reform ranging from the Education Act to the Factory Act, imperial wars, and more importantly, Irish Home Rule. By the 1890s, an empowered and increasingly enfranchised working class made inroads into the House of Commons, and various factions within the Conservative and Liberal Parties led to a weakening of the power of the ruling elite that completely broke down in the aftermath of WWI.

Chapter 2: Class in Edwardian England

The Aristocracy
The British aristocracy is divided into two components: the peerage and the landed gentry. The peerage is, as the name states, made up of peers—dukes, marquesses, earls, viscounts, and barons—and the landed gentry made up of baronets, knights, and gentlemen of no title, but of noble blood (think Mr. Darcy of *Pride and Prejudice*).

To outsiders, this gradation of social rank could be confusing: why was Mr. Darcy a gentleman, but Mr. Collins was not? Simply stated, it was because of land. Since suffrage was long tied to land ownership, and land ownership tied to inheritance or wealth, a landowner was almost always a gentleman, and a gentleman was almost always a landowner.

Because of this social truth, the first move made by the *nouveaux riche* of the late Victorian and Edwardian eras was to purchase property in the country. Anglo-Jewish magnates such as the Rothschilds and Sir Julius Wernher became just as known for their lavish country estates as they were for their wealth. Wealthy Americans, such as Bradley Martin and Andrew Carnegie, also sought to legitimize their social status with a house in the English (or Scottish) countryside—to say nothing of the manor houses built on Long Island, along the Hudson River, and in Newport.

The late Victorian and Edwardian eras were also the epoch of *Country Life* magazine, which celebrated the country pursuits and simple, bucolic life of this class. More than a decade later, British officers prized the copies of *Country Life* sent to the trenches, passing them on to one another in order to savor the stately homes, fetes, and sports they left behind. In issues of society magazines like *The Tatler* or *The Bystander*, there were also pages of advertisements listing country estates for sale or to let, thus revealing both the demand for one's own place in the country and how hard up many traditional aristocrats actually were.

This combination of private wealth and land ownership kept political power in the hands of landowners, as it was considered a gentleman's duty to represent the interests of the public and their right as wealthy, well-born, and educated. This public duty and the duty to tend to the land is why the most important tenet of the aristocracy was that a gentleman did not work. Young gentlemen were steeped in the glories of their special calling to rule from their early schooling at Eton or Harrow (Winchester, Charterhouse and Rugby were also acceptable), and it was further cemented by their time at Oxford or Cambridge, or, if desirous of an army or navy career, Sandhurst and Dartmouth, where they were automatically trained as officers.

The aristocratic lady was usually less educated than their male counterparts, but their upbringing focused on the social niceties and necessities for their future roles as political and social hostesses. Unlike the American heiresses who swooped in and filched their potential suitors, the English lady was taught to run an aristocratic household, how to deal with servants and tradesmen, and how to advance her husband's career in whichever field he so chose. Because she was bred to compliment her husband and to further the goals of her own family, young debutantes were guided only towards suitable prospects. If her family were High Tories, the only eligible men she would meet were also High Tory. If she were from a diplomatic family, marriage to another diplomat or a Foreign Office official was a foregone conclusion. Everything about her upbringing was designed to rule on some level, and shyness or shirking of duties was not tolerated.

The responsibilities of the landed gentry were on a smaller scale, but were of no less importance. In fact, county families, by dint of their year-round residence, frequently possessed greater power and influence than the local aristocratic family, who typically moved between London and their various country estates throughout the year. These were the magistrates or justices of the peace, the squires, the Masters of the Hunt, and the MPs.

The women ran the village charities, visited schools and the poor, and organized country entertainments such as church bazaars and flower shows. Granted, the wife of a mere knight or Mr. would accede precedence to the local peeress, but in the eyes of the village, Mrs. _____ was just as important as the Countess of _____.

Both pieces of the aristocracy worked in tandem to rule and reign society from the top down. They considered it their birthright and duty to lead and lead by example, though the basis of their might began to erode during the Edwardian era. Yet, the singular characteristics of the peerage and landed gentry remained a benchmark for the formation of English society, and no amount of Labour MPs or aristocratic bankruptcies could shake this.

The Peerage
The British peerage retained its influence in its simplicity and uniformity. Unlike the European peerage, which basically handed titles to each offspring, thereby diluting the exclusiveness of a title, land and titles remained mostly bound together and created a sturdier foundation for building and retaining wealth and influence.

At the top of the peerage is a *duke*. The title was first introduced by Edward III in 1337 when he created the Black Prince the first English duke. A Duke is called "Duke" or "Your Grace" by social equals, but only "Your Grace" by commoners. His eldest son bore his courtesy title, his younger sons were known as "Lord Firstname Lastname," and his daughters as "Lady Firstname Lastname."

Next is a *marquess/marquis*: This was introduced in 1387 by Richard II. A Marquess is called "My Lord" by both social equals and commoners. His eldest son also bore his courtesy title, and like a duke's other children, his younger sons are "Lord Firstname Lastname" and his daughters "Lady Firstname Lastname."

The title of *earl* was Latin for comes or comte/count in French. Before the creation of a duke, this was the highest degree of rank and dignity in the British peerage. An earl is called "My Lord" by social equals and commoners, the eldest son bore his father's courtesy title, but though the daughters are "Lady Firstname Lastname," the other sons are "Honorable Firstname Lastname."

The *viscount* is the fourth degree of rank and dignity in the British peerage, and was introduced by Henry VI in 1440. A viscount is called "My Lord" by social equals and commoners. All of his children are "Honourable Firstname Lastname." The *baron* is the lowest rank in the British peerage. A baron is called "My Lord," and all children are "Honorable Firstname Lastname."

Though a *baronet* is a hereditary rank instituted by James I in 1612, it is lower than the peerage but higher than all knights, those of the Order of the Garter the lone exception.

In matters of precedence, women took theirs from the rank and dignity of their fathers, and all unmarried sisters in any family held the same degree, which is the degree that their eldest brother held (or would hold) amongst men. For example, when the half-brother of Ottoline Morrell (née Cavendish-Bentinck) became the 6th Duke of Portland, she was granted the courtesy title of a duke's daughter, thereby becoming *Lady* Ottoline.

The Middle Classes
The middle class was stratified along a host of lines, ranging from income and profession, one's family background, where one lived, and where one was educated.

According to Alastair Service in his book *Edwardian Interiors*, the lower middle classes ranged from "clerks and shop assistants earning between £90 and £170 a year, up through several other subtle levels and occupations. Senior foremen in factories, commercial travellers, practitioners of some arts or crafts, members of some professions such as most school-teachers or surveyors, small business men—all these were grouped in the higher levels of the lower middle class and earned between £150 and £600 per annum."

The Upper middle classes were "mostly speaking English within shades of a nationwide 'educated' accent, except in the north of England, Scotland and Wales"...their occupations might be in "suitable businesses or in professions such as law or medicine, or they might be landowners. Their incomes, to maintain an ostensibly upper middle-class way of life in Edwardian times, had to be around or at least £800 and above" depending on financial success.

Each level of this class was jealous of their position, very aware that one false move—a bankruptcy, an unwanted pregnancy, a redundancy, an accident—could plunge them into poverty, or worse, a lower rung on the social ladder. The anxieties of the Edwardian middle class are apparent in E.M. Forster's best-known novels, *A Room with a View* and *Howard's End*.

Both deal with three layers of the middle class: the leisured upper middle class is represented in Cecil Vyse and the Schlegel siblings, the fastidious and climbing lower middle class by the Honeychurch family and the Wilcoxes, and the uncertain lower-lower middle class by George Emerson and Leonard Bast (and Bast hangs on the lowest rung: a clerk).

The contrast between country life and London life for the middle classes is also evident in these books, particularly in *Howards End*. The ownership of a London residence and a country house is a source of pride for Henry Wilcox, and the potential loss of Howard's End to Margaret Schlegel awakens his fear of losing both his foothold in the upper regions of the middle class and a possession.

The livelihood of the middle class was dependent upon, as stated before, income and profession, one's family background, where one lived, and where one was educated. Most of the middle class lived in cities where they worked, but they also lived in the newly created suburbs or in the spacious Garden Cities created along the aesthetics of the Arts and Crafts Movement. Some—daringly—even lived in apartment flats!

For the most part, the middle classes, barred by lack of wealth, connection, or background from most of the London Season, created their own little society within their homes: dances with gramophones or pianists rather than expensive orchestras; dramatic and operatic societies, golf, cricket, and tennis; intellectual games; and reading books by the latest writers (the middle classes were more apt to read "radical" novels than the upper and aristocratic classes).

In general, the middle class man did not attend exclusive public schools like Eton or Charterhouse, nor was he likely to go up to Oxford or Cambridge for his advanced education. Many were first educated by governesses, and then sent to kindergarten at five or six. After that, the young middle class boy attended a private or grammar school, which were often run from large private houses in the country and proclaimed to teach the sons of "Gentlemen".

The gradations in middle class society rear its head once again, for in Middle Class speak, a gentleman was a man of the professional class or a businessman, and anyone in "Trade" was excluded from this designation. The son of a builder could get into these types of school, but the son of a prosperous grocer could not.

When schooling ended, these sons of the Middle Class would enter their father's line of business, or earn their stripes as an apprentice with their father's friend, before being allowed to take up a management position in their father's company. If, however, this young man showed a marked aptitude for some other profession, such as architecture or law, their father rifled through his vast business connections to give his son a boost.

Middle class young ladies were bred to be wives, but they were fortunate in that they were allowed education and work before—or perhaps in lieu of—marriage. They, like their brothers, were educated by governesses and a kindergarten teacher, and also attended one of the numerous girls' schools founded in the 1870s and 1880s. If destined to be a typist in the City, these young ladies attended secretarial schools or took business courses, but the wider world of employment was open to them as well.

In addition, it was the Middle Class young lady who breached the masculine enclaves of Oxford and Cambridge to attend Somerville or Girton, and were taken on as equals in such places as Manchester University. The Middle Class young lady was also the pioneer in the medical profession and the teaching profession, and were from whence the formidable headmistresses of girls' schools derived.

Overall, the Edwardian middle classes were not the repressed and extremely moral types associated the Victorian era. They were less wealthy and less powerful than the aristocracy was, and a little insular in outlook, but they were surprisingly more progressive in many areas in which the aristocracy feared to tread.

The Working Class and the Poor
The lives of the Edwardian working class and poor were widely documented by Socialists, journalists, and novelists of the day.

During the Victorian era, religious leaders and literature influenced the growth of social activism for the benefit of the poor. Though the mindset of many was that poverty was the fault of the impoverished—hence the formation the workhouse—and wealth the sign of blessing, many wealthy Britons were moved to devote their time and money to helping the underclass.

Philanthropy became a sort of business, and by the end of the nineteenth century, there were scores upon scores of organizations and charities created to help a variety of indigent people, ranging from unwed mothers, to sailors' widows and children, to the blind—and many were based in London alone.

Mandatory schooling and a gradually increase in men's suffrage went hand-in-hand in creating a generation of poor who saw charity as merely the salving of an aristocrat's conscience and not genuine action to help the less fortunate. The legalization of trade unions in the 1870s gave the underclass a voice, and by the Edwardian era, the working classes had transformed from the pathetic to the political. It is here that the Labour Party was birthed, and the socialist agitation that unnerved the ruling classes.

A great majority of the working class lived, worked, and played in Britain's major cities. The best account for life in London is Charles Booth's *Life and Labour of the People in London* , whose nearly 30 volumes published between 1886 and 1903 provided an incredibly rich and detailed portrait of life for the working classes and poor of late Victorian and Edwardian London. While living in England, American author Jack London followed the example of Jacob Riis's celebrated book of underclass New York, *How the Other Half Lives*, by penning *The People of the Abyss,* his own first-hand account of life in London's East End.

London's book was well-received, but it was one of many books that fed the "better half's" insatiable desire for a glimpse of poverty. Best-seller lists of the late 1890s revealed a fad for fiction written from the perspective of the grimy, dull-eyed poor, and Stephen Crane's *Maggie: A Girl of the Streets* was popular on both side of the Atlantic. Well-to-do readers gloried in these books, and the more sordid, the better—perhaps to convince themselves that these ill-bred and derelict people could never rise above their station to challenge the social order.

In general, the lives of the working class bore a superficial resemblance to sensational novels and newspaper articles. These men and women, many of whom found work ranging from temporary labor, sweatshops, and manufacturing, to waiting on tables in good restaurants, millinery, and respectable street trades, took pride in their labors, and caught the zeitgeist of the period: change, reform, and militancy.

Their education was meager in comparison to the classes above them, and they resided in slums rather than elegant flats and country estates, nor were they as adequately fed and shod as wealthier people. However, they did wrest control over their destiny and rather than being passive acceptors of poor relief and charity, many working class men and women found their own voices and formed their own societies for the betterment of their class.

The Servant Class
Contrary to the images in period dramas, the life of a domestic servant was dreary, wearying, dirty, and often thankless. The domestic servant knew their place, and was proud to serve the grandest of houses, but their tenure in service was largely left up to a combination of their temperament and the temperament of their masters and mistresses. However, the turn of the century saw the rise of the "Servant Problem," wherein households found it difficult to obtain and retain their staff.

This was due to the increase in factories, entry-level white collar positions in department stores, and education. Male servants also became increasingly expensive to keep, and after the passing of the Workmen's Compensation Act of 1906, employers were required to pay insurance on their staff.

Despite the sprightliness of TV's fictional servants, all other details are rather accurate. In a smaller household of perhaps five or six servants, it was easier to rise in the ranks. A typical "tweeny"—a young girl of eleven or twelve assigned to the "in between" tasks of cleaning, setting fires, and assisting Cook—could rise to housemaid by age fourteen. If she so chose, she could find a position in another household, where she could be hired on as parlourmaid and waitress.

After toiling there for a few years, she would take her experience to a larger household, where she could be head housemaid at aged eighteen, and should the daughter of the house take a liking to her, become this young lady's personal maid.

Once the young lady married (say, seven years later, aged twenty-one), our former tweeny, now twenty-five, had the option of going with the newly married young lady as her personal lady's maid. Or perhaps the ambitious maid set her eye on becoming a housekeeper. If the married young lady did not marry a titled gentleman or a gentleman with a country estate, our maid could double her duties as lady's maid and pseudo-housekeeper in the London residence, thus earning twice the experience necessary for further ascension up the domestic ranks.

Perhaps her mistress attends a country house party and takes her lady's maid, whose brisk manner catches the eye of the housekeeper anxious to retire. Our lady's maid/housekeeper is then "poached" by the lady of the house, and with a "Mrs." in front of her surname and the keys to the house, the lowly eleven year old tweeny has now become a housekeeper of a grand estate. The trajectory for a male servant was rather the same, though they had less steps to take, should they rise from hallboy to footman to butler.

The First World War effectively ended the affordability of domestic servants, and only the wealthiest of households could afford just a fraction of the immense staff employed before the war. Domestic servants in the post-war era now demanded better pay and treatment, and many women, having experienced a taste of freedom in the munitions factories (and male servants jaded by the shared experience of the trenches with their masters—and seeing many of them maimed or killed), were less likely to blindly accept the yoke of being in service.

In the country, domestic service did continue to dominate the employment opportunities for farm girls and boys, but the exodus of would-be servants from this field began in the early 1900s, and the lifestyle of the leisured class changed drastically to suit this decline in available employees.

Chapter 3: The Social Round

English society was and remains a country-based society, and during the reign of Charles I, a trip to London after six to eight months or more on an estate was considered a treat. The status of London as the center of all that was licentious, amusing, and lavish became fact during the Restoration. Soon Town Houses appeared in the West End, pleasure gardens were erected in open spaces, theatres filled, and play became serious business.

During the reign of Queen Anne, the season was rather short. According to G. M. Trevelyan's *English Social History*, "The London season was over by the first week in June when people of fashion dispersed to their country homes or adjourned to Bath. A longer residence in town would have ruined many families who had strained a point to bring their daughters to the London marriage market."

As the eighteenth century wore on, the growth in power of politicians and courtiers around the Hanoverian dynasty formed the nucleus of the Season's function and purpose: London, the focal point of the burgeoning British Empire, was *the* place to see and be seen, and more pleasures sprang up around this exclusive group of aristocrats. Mothers anxious to marry their daughters recognized the convening of society provided ample opportunities to place them on display, and statesmen and courtiers—the eligible marriage partners—were also in need of entertainment.

For the most of the eighteenth century, the Season was exclusive to the few hundred aristocratic families of England. Everyone knew one another, or knew of one another, and outsiders were rarely permitted entry. Because of this assurance of rank and blood, Society lived, ate, and played in public. They had no need to hide their rituals from the general public because no merchant or shopkeeper would ever have the opportunity to mingle with them or ape their mores and manners. This changed during the Industrial Revolution, which saw the growth of the middle class and the creation of non-landed millionaires practically overnight.

When the prosperous middle class clamored for a voice in politics, and more horrifying, a place in the social round, the reaction of the aristocracy was to close ranks. Their amusements and entertainments now took place behind closed doors, where the middle classes, who hoped to copy the way they dressed, spoke, ate, and played in effort to acquire "gentility" could not see them.

After all, should these *nouveaux riches* acquire the habits deemed aristocratic, one could not tell a gentleman and a greengrocer's son apart.

The middle class then turned to the example set by Queen Victoria and her large family. During the early decades of her reign, Queen Victoria shrewdly used "social media"—illustrated newspapers, magazines, photography, official portraits, and public sightings—to recreate the mystique and awe of the Royal Family lost under the reign of Mad King George and his profligate sons. The Royal Family and its doings were now accessible to the curious middle and lower classes, but on Victoria's terms.

However, the secluded aristocracy grew bored with middle-class respectability, and though there were some rebels (the fast and beautiful Duchess of Manchester aroused the ire of Queen Victoria in the 1850s), they had to wait until the Prince of Wales came of age to indulge in the raucous amusements and lavish display of the past.

Yet, throughout these changes, and even into the Edwardian era, when society had expanded to include the wealthy financiers and plutocrats despised eighty years before, the importance of the Season continued to lay in its role of uniting the country's leading families for social, political, and marital contacts.

The London Season
Court festivities and functions had always had an influence on the season, but when Queen Victoria came to the throne, the London season became fixed upon the social calendar: the meeting of Parliament in February marked its beginning, it was at its fullest during Whitsuntide (or Pentecost) saw it at its fullest, and the onset of the summer heat in July marked its ending. Many key events of the Season, particularly the sporting events, were well in place before the Victorian era, but never did they all function in tandem.

During the early years of Queen Victoria's married life, state functions followed one another at a rapid pace, with fancy dress balls, banquets, and dramatic representations at Windsor Castle filling her days. The Derby and Ascot, with its State procession, were the great sporting events of the London Season, and the opera at Covent Garden and plays at the principal London theatres, were other highlights. After Victoria's seclusion after the death of Prince Albert, the social calendar she had ushered in was supported by the Prince and Princess of Wales (and his siblings and their spouses to a lesser degree) and the aristocracy.

The official opening of the Season was the Private View at the Royal Academy in May. The Royal Academy was formed in 1769 when a group of artists asked George III to give his blessing to an academy that would teach painting and exhibit it. Prior to this, art was the sole province of the wealthy and the royal: there were no public art galleries, artists worked at the discretion of their patrons, and only the privileged could get in to see a private or royal collection. The first show took place in a hired room in Pall Mall and contained only 136 pictures. One hundred years later, when the Royal Academy moved to Burlington House, there were 4,500 works submitted.

From an American viewpoint in 1910:

> "It is not private and there isn't any view, so far as pictures are concerned. On the previous days the noble rooms opening one out of another seem practically empty, and a dense silence prevails. Greetings between the newspaper men are few and carried on in whispers. Each of those present is confronted with serious work, and he edges along the colored walls, notebook in one hand and pencil in the other, with a catalogue tucked under his arm, writing down the points for his article in on today's paper.
>
> The man privileged to enter Burlington House on press day enjoys the real Private View of that year's pictures. He crosses the broad courtyard of Burlington House quite unimpeded by any vehicle, climbs the broad, deserted stairs, where the dignified attendant in uniform clips the right-hand corner from his card of admission, and hands him a large-leaved copy of the catalogue, for which he does not pay—and after that he owns the building.
>
> Vastly different is the sight on Saturday. The courtyard is packed with buzzing automobiles, splendid carriages, an so on down the list of equipages until we reach the humble hansom cab. The police in attendance are busy speeding the parting motor to make room for the next. Wide as the stairs are, the dense procession must mount slowly. At the top there is no more clipping of tickets, for the cards are taken up and flung into a waste-basket. The rooms are packed like gigantic sardine boxes, and a roar resembling that of Babel echoes down from the roof, for everyone is laughing and talking, and the silent, unnoticed pictures enjoy a private view of the world's celebrities."

Next in importance was the opening night of Covent Garden's opera season. An enduring vision of this night can be seen in the opening scenes of *My Fair Lady*, where Eliza Doolittle tries to sell her last bunches of flowers—for Covent Garden was London's key flower market—to the toffs waiting out the rain. The Royal Opera House had undergone multiple renovations, mostly related to fires, and it was where the choicest operas, ballets, and orchestras performed.

The patroness of Coven Garden was Lady de Grey, who plucked Nellie Melba from relative obscurity to become the prima donna of Edwardian opera. It was considered *de rigueur* to attend the opera in full evening dress, with ladies in their most glittering tiaras. Lady de Grey also brought the Ballet Russes to London. She saw them perform their erotic, unsettling ballet in 1907, and was determined to get them to England. She had an uphill battle against prejudices, since ballet was considered either part of music hall entertainment or a backdrop to the opera. The Ballet Russes were art unto themselves, and when they finally made their debut at Covent Garden in 1911, audiences were electrified.

After the month of May, the great social events revolved sport—Ascot, Derby, Henley, Cowes, and Goodwood—but sandwiched in between them were luncheons, military reviews, dinners, dances, flower shows, concerts, matinees, afternoon "At Homes," polo, tennis, court balls and concerts, rides in Hyde Park, four-in-hand meets, cricket matches, House of Common teas, and evening fetes. Charitable events, such as bazaars, subscription dinners, fundraisers, and appearances, also filled the season to the brim.

Of the greatest sporting events of the season, the Derby was the most democratic. Perhaps it is the result of its founding as a lark by an aristocrat rather than founded by a royal, but when Derby Day came in early June, the sun shone brightly on the heads of prostitutes, costermongers, dukes, sailors, and princes alike. In the 1850s, Charles Dickens noted the gigantic amount of food available at the refreshment saloon: 2400 tumblers, 1200 wine glasses, 3000 plates and dishes...130 legs of lamb, 65 saddles of lamb, 20 rounds of beef, 500 spring chickens, 350 pigeon pies, and a large quantity of quartern loaves and ham for sandwiches.

Queen Victoria visited Derby once in 1840, but it was her son, the Prince of Wales, who found the race to his liking. He attended every year and entered horses from his stud, and when his own Persimmon won the Derby in 1896, cries of "Good Old Teddy!" could be heard from the diverse crowd.

The most infamous Derby Day was in 1913, when suffragette Emily Davison threw herself in front of the King's horse, and when the horse of C. Bowyer Ismay, brother of Titanic's J. Bruce Ismay, was mysteriously disqualified after winning the race.

The aristocratic Ascot came next. Inaugurated by Queen Anne in 1711, whose plate of 100 guineas were very high stakes for the time, this event was grand and showy, where the men wore grey morning dress and a silk topper and the women wore their best summer frocks and most elaborate hats.

The Royal Procession to the Royal Enclosure, to which only the choicest of aristocrats were invited, capped the event. Viscount Churchill, whose job it was to select those suitable for invitation, dropped applications into three baskets marked Certainly, Perhaps, and Certainly Not.

In the mid-nineteenth century, Ascot was the least raffish of all racecourses, and the middle classes, equipped with their own lovely carriages, also came to see and be seen. It was said the best horses were shown at Ascot, and the prettiest women, and the magnetism of the race was so strong, eighteen days after the Armistice was signed in 1918, bookies were already asking what horses would be raced in 1919. Edward VII left his mark on Ascot as well: the famous Black Ascot of 1910 was in his honor after his death in May.

The Henley Royal Regatta was a leisurely "river carnival" on the Thames. It was at heart a rowing race first staged in 1839 for amateur oarsmen, but soon became another fixture on the social calendar. Bungalows and houses hugging the Thames were let to spectators, and the evenings were capped by boat parties and punts, the air filled with military brass bands, and illuminated by Chinese lanterns. Dress code was strict: men in collars, ties, and jackets—though garishly-colored socks and ties were the mode—and women in crisp summer frocks and hats and parasols.

Boating clubs had their own exclusive enclosures, which kept the middle class spectators out. Since the regatta was open to non-British rowing teams, the event was known for its American element, and the Stars and Stripes were seen regularly fluttering from house boats along the river. Henley was also perfect for courting, for young men and women were permitted to man their own punts for punting parties and picnics. One can almost picture the romantic scene that could kindle a proposal of marriage.

Next on the social calendar was Goodwood. This race was founded in 1801 when the 3rd Duke of Richmond and Gordon gave members of the Goodwood Hunt permission to run a number of two-mile heats. The following year saw the first public Goodwood race-meeting, when sixteen races were run in three days for the £1001 prize-money. The Duke once hosted the Prince of Wales for the week of "Glorious Goodwood", and other aristocrats followed in his wake to set up their own house parties.

The relative inaccessibility of Goodwood made the race somewhat exclusive, though the advent of the motorcar changed this. The complexity of the racecourse made winning a feat to brag about, but Goodwood never achieved the mass popular of Ascot and the Derby.

Cowes Week in August was the last hurrah for the London season. The regatta was founded in the 1820s by George IV (the former Prince Regent), but it became popular when Queen Victoria and Prince Albert sought a home away from the stresses of court life and purchased Osborne House on the Isle of Wight in 1845. The Royal family spent a lengthy period of time on the Isle of Wight each year, so it was no surprise that Society followed them there during the summer. The Royal Yacht Squadron was a natural extension of Britain's might on the seas, and Cowes was less a time for amusement than it was for showing off the latest yachts and ships in England's arsenal via maneuvers and races.

Later on the 19th century, the conflict between the Prince of Wales and his nephew Kaiser Wilhelm manifested itself in a bitter rivalry over whose boat was the largest, swiftest, and most up-to-date.

This rivalry was also the cause of a humiliating scene: the Kaiser and Prince of Wales ignored the Queen's signal for supper in order to finish their race, and when they finally arrived at Osborne, the Kaiser laughed at his grandmother's disapproval as the Prince of Wales hid behind a pillar. Finally, when the Kaiser arrived with his latest and most advanced version of his yacht Meteor, the Prince of Wales retired from competing with his bombastic nephew and sold his yacht. Then as now, the purchasing and upkeep of a yacht was enormously expensive, and once more see an influx of wealthy Americans.

In fact, Cowes is where Lord Randolph Churchill first spied the darkly attractive Jennie Jerome in 1873 and immediately proposed marriage. No doubt it was with this romantic occasion in mind that she declared in her 1908 memoirs, "Ever since those early days Cowes has always had so great an attraction for me that, notwithstanding its gradual deterioration, I have rarely missed a yearly visit."
On the twelfth of August—the Glorious Twelfth—the Season was officially at an end and society abandoned London for country pursuits.

The Social Calendar
JANUARY
- Race meetings are held at Newmarket, Gatwick, Windsor and elsewhere
- Pheasant shooting closes at the end of the month

FEBRUARY
- Sandown Park races in Surrey
- Quorn Hunt in Leicestershire
- The Waterloo Cup–the premiere event of the hare-coursing year

MARCH
- The Grand National, the most valuable National Hunt horse race in the world

APRIL
- Parliament adjourns for Whitsuntide
- Oxford versus Cambridge boat race
- Opening of The "Oval" for Summer season (cricket)
- Primrose Day (April 19th), anniversary of the death of Benjamin Disraeli, 1st Earl of Beaconsfield
- Races at Epsom and Sandown

MAY
- Private View at the Royal Academy, the traditional starting signal of the London season
- Court drawing rooms (Moved to June, and in the evening, in Edward VII's reign)
- First night of Covent Garden's opera season
- Royal Horticultural Society's Great Flower Show

JUNE
- The Derby
- The Fourth of June at Eton
- Crystal Palace Horse Show
- Ascot Week
- Fete & gymkhana at the Ranelagh Club

JULY
- Cricket matches at Lord's; Harrow vs. Eton, Oxford vs. Cambridge
- Henley Regatta
- Goodwood race-meeting

AUGUST
- Cowes week on Isle of Wight
- Glorious Twelfth, grouse hunting on the moors of Scotland
- Stag-hunting season begins in Devon

SEPTEMBER

- Partridge season begins
- Scottish social season in Edinburgh
- Cubbing begins with the Beadle Hounds
- Races at Doncaster

OCTOBER
- Cubbing in Ireland
- Aristocratic weddings in London

NOVEMBER
- Hunting season begins
- Country Ball season

DECEMBER
- Christmas in the country
- Boxing Day (Dec. 26)
- Twelfth Night celebrations (Twelve days of Christmas: Dec 25-Jan 6)

Chapter 4: London, A Sprawling Metropolis

At the time of Queen Victoria's death, London had transformed from merely the capitol of Great Britain, to the pulse of an Empire. Inside a scant 120 square miles resided the wealthiest and the poorest, the modern and the ancient, and every strata of society from royalty down to the humblest flower girl. London was also where bankers, financiers, politicians, and Cabinet ministers directed the money and administration of a people spread across many lands and made up of many tongues and religions. During the Edwardian era, the drastic change that characterized 19th century London had slowed a bit, but the population did not, growing from 4,536,063 persons in 1901 to 4,872,700 in 1910.

Baedeker's *London* describes Edwardian London thusly:

The definition of "London" had two meanings: the Administrative County of London, including the City and the districts more directly under the jurisdiction of the London County Council, and Greater London, or the district of the Metropolitan and City Police. The latter extended 12-15 miles in every direction from Charing Cross, which embraced an area of 700 sq. M., with a population estimated in 1910 at 7,537,000. London was halved by the flow of the Thames into two areas: north (Middlesex) and south (Surrey and Kent), with the former being of less importance (Southwark, Lambeth, Greenwich, etc).

The Middlesex portion of London was also halved:

I. The City and the East End, consisting of the part of London that lay to the East of the Temple, and formed the commercial and money-making quarter of the Metropolis. It embraced the Port, the Docks, the Custom House, the Bank, the Exchange, the innumerable counting-houses of merchants, moneychangers, brokers, and underwriters, the General Post Office, the printing and publishing offices of The Times, the legal corporations of the Inns of Court, and the Cathedral of St. Paul's.

II. The West End, consisting of the part of London that lay to the West of the Temple, was the quarter of London that spent money, made laws, and regulated the fashions. It contained Buckingham Palace, the mansions of the aristocracy, the clubs, museums, picture galleries, theatres, army barracks, government offices, Houses of Parliament, and Westminster Abbey; and it was the special locality for parks, squares, and gardens.

Then, London was divided into areas known for particular trades or social class:

I. East End and South London

1. Long Shore, which extends along the bank of the Thames, and is chiefly composed of quays, wharves, storehouses, and engine-factories, and inhabited by shipwrights, lightermen, sailors, and marine store dealers.
2. Whitechapel, with its Jewish tailoring workshops.
3. Houndsditch and the Minories, the quarters of the Jews.
4. Bethnal Green and Spitalfields to the N., and part of Shoreditch, form a manufacturing district, once occupied to a large extent by silk-weavers, partly descended from the French Protestants (Huguenots) who took refuge in England after the Revocation of the Edict of Nantes in 1685. Furniture-making and boot-making are now the chief industries.
5. Clerkenwell, between Islington and Hatton Garden, the district of watch-makers and metal-workers.
6. Paternoster Row, near St. Paul's Cathedral, the focus of the book-trade.

7. Chancery Lane and the Inns of Court, the headquarters of barristers, solicitors, and law-stationers.
8. Wapping, Shadwell, Limehouse, Poplar, and MUlwall, all chiefly composed of quays, wharves, storehouses, and engine-factories, and inhabited by shipwrights, lightermen, sailors, and marine store dealers.
9. Southwark and Lambeth, containing numerous potteries, glass-works, machine-factories, breweries, and hop-warehouses.
10. Bermondsey, famous for its tanneries, glue-factories, and wool-warehouses.
11. Rotherhithe, farther to the E., chiefly inhabited by sailors, ship-carpenters, coal-heavers, and bargemen.
12. Deptford, with its great cattle-market.
13. Greenwich, with its hospital, park, and observatory.
14. Woolwich, with its arsenal and barracks.

II. West End

1. Mayfair, aristocratic neighborhood
2. Belgravia, aristocratic neighborhood, but less exclusive
3. Westminster & St James's, the administrative and royal boroughs
4. Kensington, upper middle class, though marked by Kensington Palace
5. Bayswater, middle class neighborhood
6. Pimlico, part of Belgravia
7. The Strand, theatres, restaurants, and Fleet Street
8. Chelsea, a bit Bohemian
9. Brompton, with the South Kensington Museums
10. Bloomsbury, boarding houses for university students, the British Museum.

Center of the Empire
The aorta of the British Empire lay in Westminster. In it lay Buckingham Palace, Westminster Abbey, and other offices vital to the official, diplomatic, and legislative functions necessary to keeping everything running in shipshape and Bristol fashion. During the Queen's reign, Buckingham Palace was only used for state ceremonies, since Victoria preferred

Windsor Castle. When Edward VII came to the throne, he cleared Buckingham Palace of its decades of clutter and neglect and turned it into the centerpiece of his glittering court. Though the palace eventually came to symbolize the British monarchy, it was only built in the 1820s during the reign of George IV, and only made the official London residence of the monarch—as mentioned above—under Edward VII.

According to a description in 1901:

> "Buckingham Palace is splendid inside, much more so than most people imagine, and can hold its own in point of magnificence with anything of its kind abroad. The vestibule, into which the Sovereign's entrance in the quadrangle opens, and the grand marble staircase with its ormolu acanthus balustrades, are very imposing; as are also the state apartments—the throne-room with its splendid ceiling, huge crystal chandelier, and emblazoned arms; the grand saloon; the state dining-room; the handsome Bow Room; the green, yellow and blue drawing-rooms; and the picture-gallery, a noble apartment in the centre of the Palace with gorgeously-gilded door-cases and with four marble chimneypieces elaborately sculptured with medallion portraits of great painters.
>
> There is a fine collection of pictures here, and, indeed, all over the Palace, only surpassed by that at Windsor Castle, where every square foot of available wall-space is covered by them. In the Dutch and Flemish school, the Buckingham Palace collection is remarkably rich—Rembrandt, Rubens, Teniers, Ostade, Cuyp, Gerard Dow, and Van Dyck, etc. Amongst the numerous English painters represented, Wilkie is well to the front, and there are endless Royal portraits by Kneller, Lely, Lawrence, Angeli, Winterhalter, etc. Like the Bow Room, the lower dining-hall overlooks the gardens and terrace, and is one of the cosiest apartments in the Palace. White and gold form the basis of the decorative treatment, and numerous oil-paintings hang on the walls, including portraits of Queen Anne, George III.,

his Queen, Caroline, King Frederick I. of Prussia, etc., and a wonderful picture by Stanfield of the opening of London Bridge in 1831 by William IV.

The grandest thing in the Palace, is perhaps the ball-room. It is nobly proportioned, lighted from above by electricity, and from the sides by handsome gilt-bronze candelabra. Its ceiling is richly decorated; the walls are panelled in crimson silk; and the floor is beautifully inlaid with oak. When a state concert is in progress, its appearance is striking in the extreme. On either side are three tiers of seats facing those on the floor-level, all occupied by most brilliantly-attired personages, for on these occasions the most beautiful dresses and jewels are worn. At the upper end of the room is the organ (originally at the Brighton Pavilion) ; on one side of the platform is a right royal-looking harp, and on the other a fine Brard Grand, ornamented with richly gilt scroll-work."

Buckingham Palace's gardens, some forty acres in size, was the sight of splendid garden parties, which was nearly the only time the "public" (that is, those not in the highest circles of society—doctors, lawyers, scientists, etc) could meet or mingle with the Queen. Use of the palace was not restricted to the reigning monarch, however, and many family members resided in the block of private apartments allotted for royal guests.

The Palace of St. James's was of less importance, though many state functions generally for male guests, were held here. As befitting the London home of the monarch, all major roads in the West End lead from Buckingham Palace—The Mall to Trafalgar Square, Constitution Hill to Piccadilly at Hyde Park Corner, Buckingham Palace Road to Belgravia, and Birdcage Walk into the heart of the Government.

"Whitehall" was the metonym for the area in which lay the Foreign Office, Home Office, the Houses of Parliament, the

Treasury, the Admiralty, and Scotland Yard. The name derived from the old Palace of Whitehall, which burnt down in 1698. Number 10, Downing Street, the residence of the Prime Minister, and No. 11—the office of the Chancellor of the Exchequer—were of little architectural consequence, but on the ground floor of No. 10 was the Council Chamber where the Prime Minister discussed matters of grave importance with the Cabinet.

The Foreign Office was approached from Downing Street, and "inside were the great apartments—Cabinet Council room, conference rooms, reception rooms, etc.—, the Library, where every book or pamphlet bearing upon Foreign Office affairs was to be found, and suites of pleasantly situated rooms, devoted to interviews with Ambassadors, the Diplomatic Corps generally, and the Consular section of the Foreign Office. Other apartments are the sanctuaries of Chiefs of Departments, Heads of sub-divisions, and their staffs, etc., where is transacted a vast amount of real business, the routine work alone being very heavy."

A square tower facing St. James' Park marked the separation of the building of the Foreign Office from the India Office. "Here, too, there is a splendid library, whose shelves quickly reveal that this Department directs a Great Eastern Empire. Indian curios in the chief offices, and a certain air of dignified languor in the officials themselves, make the fact more apparent." Going up Downing Street was the Colonial Office, where "the Crown's authority, such as it is, over the self-governing colonies, is exercised, and Governors are nominated."

There also existed the office of the Crown Agents for the colonies, who managed the affairs of such British possessions as the West Indies, Straits Settlements, etc, and the Emigrants' Information Bureau.

The Admiralty was also in Whitehall, where naval matters were overseen, and further down the way was the War Office in Pall Mall, which handled army matters (and both sections were very jealous of one another—their respective secrecy was one of the factors that hurt the British military during the early stages of WWI). There was also Somerset House, where taxes were handled, the Wills and Probate Office, the Custom House, and the various agencies of Dominion colonies (Australia, Canada, New Zealand, etc).

Westminster Abbey was separate from the Palace of Westminster, or Houses of Parliament, but both existed on the same plot of land. Big Ben and its spires are iconic, but they were only built in 1834, after the old Palace was destroyed by fire. Inside lay the two houses—Commons and Lords—, galleries, chambers, and even a restaurant.

High Society
The smartest and only addresses for aristocratic society were in Mayfair and Belgravia. St. James's was also a residential district, capped by the extremely smart and elegant row of terraced mansions on Carlton House Terrace, which was built over the site of the Prince Regent's Carlton House, and the London mansions of the Earl Spencer, the Earl of Ellesmere, and the Marquess of Stafford. However, it was primarily known as clubland, for this is where the great political, sporting, social, and military clubs had their residence.
A list of these clubs would take up an entire section, but these are the primary ones: Carlton, 94 Pall Mall, the premier Conservative Club; Brooks's. 60 St. James's St. (Whig/Liberal club); Army and Navy, 36 Pall Mall; Guards', 70 Pall Mall; Automobile, Pall Mall; Boodle's, 28 St. James's St. (chiefly for country gentlemen); Marlborough, 52 Pall Mall; Travellers', 106 Pall Mall (where each member must have travelled at least 1000 miles from London); and White's, 37 St. James's Street.

The most favored shopping district of aristocratic London was Bond Street. Untainted by the department stores in Knightsbridge or Brompton, Bond Street—divided into New and Old—remained dominated by exclusive shops where goods were elegant and costly, service discreet and obsequious, and where one needn't leave anything but a card with the shopkeeper once you had chosen all you desired.

Young ladies were never permitted to shop alone, and even married ladies were required to take a footman with them, who would carry packages, open doors, and man the carriage. And best yet, Bond Street refused to bow to the motorcar fashion. Well into the Edwardian era, the street was free of the tuff-tuff and petrol of the automobile—though not free of the "droppings" left behind by horses.

Off Bond Street were a number of ladies' clubs—a late Victorian invention—which were perfectly placed for the well-to-do lady to drop in after a busy afternoon's shopping for a cup of tea or a hand of bridge.

In the mid-1900s, couture came to London, and when Paquin, Worth, and Doucet opened London branches (though, mostly for the wealthy Americans living in London, since many aristocratic women preferred to have their lady's maids copy the latest modes), the old, reliable court dressmakers were forced to smarten up or be left in the nineteenth century.

Savile Row tailoring, however, remained the pinnacle of menswear, and even Parisian gentlemen traveled to London at least once in their life to be measured by the best London tailors. Also in Bond Street were hatters and milliners, purveyors of women's underclothing, furriers, shoemakers, opticians, and makers of waterproof goods.

The tents of High Society required these "uniforms," so to speak, in order to mark one another as members of the same tribe. Another mark was the appearance at Hyde Park during the fashionable hours for riding (8 am to 12 pm) and driving (5-7 pm), and the Sunday Church parade (1-2 pm).

Middle Class
Middle class London was less lavish, but no less exciting than high society life. The wealthier middle class lived in

Kensington and Bayswater, in nice mansions and apartment flats, and the less wealthy tended to live in St. John's Wood or around Regent's Park. London's wealthy Jewish popular also lived in or near these areas, with Maida Vale being a particular enclave. Since the middle classes lived and played indoors, it was perhaps fitting that their areas of residence were mostly filled with houses, apartment blocks, and villas—though the great stores of Whiteley's and Harrods sprawled across large swaths of land.

Other middle-class areas were Chelsea and Bloomsbury, though both, with venerable museums in their boundaries, were considerably more bohemian in tone than the more staid areas mentioned above. The latter was home to the British Museum, whereas the former was home to the Tate Gallery and the Victoria and Albert Museum (though this was more in Brompton than in Chelsea). Chelsea was also the home of Thomas and Jane Carlyle, and a group that included Virginia Woolf's father turned their home into a museum.

Now that Woolf has been mentioned, one cannot leave out the Bloomsbury Group, who, though mostly associated with the 1920s, had its roots in the 1900s when Virginia and Vanessa Stephens purchased a house at 46 Gordon Square after the death of their father. The group gelled in or around 1910 (to quote Virginia: "on or about December 1910, human character changed"). The Edwardian era was where they all fermented, and the dichotomies of the age were very apparent in their group.

London at Play
Edwardian London was a playground not merely for the idle rich. From theatres and halls, to parks, to restaurants and chop houses, to exhibitions, to bands, to the trooping of the colors, to sports, to great events, there was no end to amusements at the reach of just about every resident. The theatre was the most democratic amusement of all, with London boasting 30 west end theatres, about 20 suburban theatres, and about 60 regular music-halls.

The most popular of these were Drury Lane, famed for the electrifying performances of Garrick, Kean, the Kembles, and Mrs. Siddons; the Gaiety Theatre (post-1903), where George Edwardes' "Gaiety Girls" became the leading attraction; the Lyceum, for popular drama; the Prince of Wales, for comedies; Haymarket, for Shakespeare with Mr. Beerbohm Tree; and the Empire and the Alhambra, both on Leicester Square, and famed for their spectacles and elaborate ballets.

Also crowding London were the numerous places to eat. The West End was where the choicest and chicest restaurants lay, mostly in the top hotels like the Savoy, the Ritz, or Claridge's, where excellent French cuisine was served. Good English cookery could be found at Simpson's-in-the-Strand, the Old Cheshire Cheese, or the chop houses in the City. Soho was where one could find cheap Italian and French restaurants, which were popular spots after the theatre, and there were also a fair number of Chinese, Indian, and German restaurants. For the less wealthy, or less discriminating, oyster shops abounded, where for a few shillings, one could down as many oysters as one could consume.

In the late Victorian era, consciousness of the poor and disadvantaged inspired the creation of parks across London. In their zeal to create these spaces, many ancient cemeteries were torn up, the graves moved elsewhere, and grass, trees, and bandstands planted in their stead. A bit morbid, but for Londoners who rarely saw greenery, much less an open space, these parks were gratefully received.

The popularity of exhibitions saw the founding of Earls Court in the Kensington area, which hosted The Empire of India Exhibition in 1896, The Victorian Era Exhibition in 1897, The Military Exhibition in 1901, Paris in London Exhibition in 1902, the International Fire Exhibition in 1903, Venice by Night in 1904 and the Imperial Austrian Exhibition in 1906. There was also the White City in Hammersmith & Fulham, where the 1908 Summer Olympics were hosted. Sunday afternoons were key times for visiting these parks and open spaces, and Londoners of different backgrounds played cricket or football to the sound of the band playing in the bandstand.

The City

In many books set in London, it is usual to see many characters refer to the city as "Town." This is because The City, or the financial district, was the whole of medieval London (and its traditional boundaries were that of the wall constructed by the Romans).

The heart of the City was the Bank of England at Threadneedle Street, from which radiated seven streets, each possessing their own metonym. Of them, Lombard Street was synonymous with banking, and was similar in might to Wall Street in New York or the Bourse in Paris. Lombard was also the home of NM Rothschild & Sons, and Lombard also became synonymous with the rich and powerful English branch of the Rothschild family, though there were over thirty great banking houses on Lombard alone.

A great description of the City is found in George Sims' *Living London*:

> "It is midday, and London's business is at high tide. Those whose working hours commence at eight o'clock, nine o'clock, and ten o'clock have all by this time got into the swing of the day's work. Shoppers and leisurely sightseers add to the throng. At innumerable stages, up to four, five, and six miles away, towards every point of the compass, omnibuses have filled at their conductors' cry, "Bank! Bank!" Through great stress of traffic have they come, and hither in long, uninterrupted processions do they continue to come. Of all colours are they, and so closely ranged together that they blot out of view all but the upper portions of the buildings. At the will of traffic-managing policemen, now this stream of vehicles, now that, holds the field.
>
> ...You are now in the money region, the land of stocks and shares. Close by are the Stock Exchange, the Royal Exchange, and a remarkable gathering together of

banks. Here the throng, representative of the district, contains a big proportion of men who deal on exchanges or are employed in the banks. The glossy hats, the well-conditioned black coats and trousers, the expensive waist. ...Through the great glass doors you see rows of busy clerks. Across the street dart young men carrying account-books or a bag secured to their person by a heavy chain. If the thousands of busy feet do not actually tread on gold, you have a feeling that underneath are vaults and strong rooms guarding fabulous hoards.

The Lord Mayor is sovereign in the City, and upon his election to the post, he is conveyed through the streets in a State coach, accompanied by aldermen, City officials, military music, and cars emblematical of their trades. He represented, figuratively and politically, the interests of the businesses and people of the City, and was treated with as much pomp as the actual Sovereign. The Lord Mayor takes "precedence of every subject of the Crown, not excepting members of the reigning house, and holds a quasi-Royal position. By virtue of his office he is head of the City Lieutenancy, and recommends the names of persons to fill vacancies. He is ex-officio chairman of the Thames Conservancy and a trustee of St. Paul's Cathedral; he has power to close or grant the use of the Guildhall; and the Company of which he is a member has precedence over all the other City companies during his year of office.

He is expected to partake of the hospitality of most of the Companies and Corporation committees, and is much in request at public gatherings of all kinds both in suburban London and in the provinces. On Sunday he sometimes attends charity sermons in state, most of the City churches being provided with a sword rest attached to the Lord Mayor's pew. Then there is the Spital sermon at Christ Church, Newgate Street, also official duties in connection with Queen Anne's Bounty and the Sons of the Clergy Corporation, and attendance at St. Paul's to meet his Majesty's judges.

> The State functions and privileges of the Lord Mayor are many and varied. He receives the password of the Tower of London quarterly under the sign manual of the Sovereign. He is entitled to venison warrants, under which he has from the Royal forests two does in midwinter and two bucks in the late summer or autumn. No troops may pass through the City without the consent of the Lord Mayor being first obtained; but the regiments descended from the Trained Bands have the right to march through with colours flying and bayonets fixed."

Besides the financial district, the Lord Mayor was aligned with the legal community of the Inns of Court and the Central Criminal Courts. The former was built on the site of the infamous Newgate prison, which was demolished in 1902 after seven hundred years of existence. The Law Courts, which stretched from the Victoria Embankment to Clerkenwell, were office, residence, and court.

From Arthur Beavan's *Imperial London*, we have a general portrait of the court:

> "English jurisprudence has been largely reformed, and the Judicature Act has created almost a revolution in legal procedure since the late Queen ascended the throne, but very few changes have taken place in the general appearance and personality of a civil tribunal. There are no Serjeants-at-law, the last of the rank and file of the ancient order of the coif, Mr. Serjeant Spinks, Q.C., having died in 1899; but the K.C.'s "silk" still occupy the front row of seats facing the Judges, while the gentlemen in stuff gowns are accommodated in the rear.
>
> From a bench in a space below the level of the barristers, still called the "well" of the Court, the attorneys continue when necessary to whisper instructions to their counsel, and there occasionally sit their clients, as did Mr. Pickwick during the hearing of the immortal Bardell v. Pickwick case. One notable change, however, there is:—no mere spectators are allowed in the body of the Court, but are relegated to

the gallery. The witness-boxes still retain their resemblance to railed-in pulpits; the jury are still cooped up in the most uncomfortable kind of pews that the wit of man can devise.

At the opening of the Courts, the Judges, bewigged and robed, emerge from little doors at the side of the dais, and take their seats beneath an emblazoned canopy, "all ranged a terrible show "; their benches being specially protected from errant currents of air by a complicated system of screens and curtains. In a little pew, with note-books before them, sit a group of individuals easily recognizable as reporters to the press, but, unlike the shabby gentlemen of a similar profession described by Dickens as generally neither neat about the cuffs or buttons, there is nothing in their dress or personal appearance to differentiate them from other people. Electric light has, however, taken the place of oil-lamps, candles, or gas that once served only to accentuate the gloom of a November day; but whether, as the late G. A. Sala maintained, the amalgamated effluvium of stuff gowns, mouldy parchments, calf bound law-books, and horse-hair wigs, is still an unmistakable characteristic of law courts, is a point every visitor must decide for himself.

The Judges have a quiet and comfortable entrance of their own in Carey Street, and robing-rooms and private apartments, where during the luncheon interval they can enjoy the traditional chop and glass or two of dry sherry, and refresh themselves for further labours. Their working hours are said to average twenty-eight and a half in a week, and those who are aware of the very onerous and trying nature of judicial duties would hardly desire to increase them. We also have it on the authority of Mr. Justice Bucknill, that although he was not sorry to be a Judge, 'it was a rather dreary life.'"

The East End

Last, but not least, we come to the East End. As stated in the beginning, the "East End" is a catch-all phrase for numerous neighborhoods known for particular trades. In fact, there were pockets of poverty across London, and one could find a workhouse tucked even in the corner of Mayfair (there was one just off Berkeley Square).

Far from being uniformly poor and downtrodden, the people of the East End ranged from working class to working poor to habitually unemployed to underemployed—essentially, just like today's lower class.

The 1890s saw the clearing of the Victorian rookeries—and also the airing of the aristocratic slum lords like Lord Colebrooke and Lady Kinloss of the Old Nichol rookery—for the construction of sanitary housing and council flats. The East End was also the site of settlement homes, in particular Toynbee Hall, all of whom were founded by civic-minded college graduates and vicars, who strove to improve the lives of the poor while living among them (as opposed to dispensing charity and returning to one's mansion).

The settlement house movement caught fire across Britain and came to America—and Jane Addams' Hull House in Chicago remains one of the most famous settlement houses in the United States.

I shall leave you with another of Arthur Beavan's descriptions, this time of a typical East End neighborhood:
> "The houses are chiefly one story, or at the most two stories high; the shops, small, and such as minister solely to the necessities of life: butchers', who deal in cheap New Zealand mutton and inferior beef; fishmongers', whose stock-in-trade is of uncertain age, with mussels and whelks, and every kind of dried fish well to the fore; pork-butchers', and ham-and-beef shops, generally of superior size, and well patronized; "purveyors" of cow-heel and ox-cheek, of tripe and trotters, their windows innocent of provisions until the day's "boiling" or "dressing" is accomplished, then overflowing with these popular dainties; fried-fish

shops, very much to the front up to all hours of the night; and general-dealers, who sell anything from firewood to tinned salmon; public-houses, of course, but of a subdued order, with plate-glass, paint, and gilding waiting to be renewed.

Should the back-street happen to have no regular shops, there is still business done. Numerous parlour-windows demonstrate the nature of the retail-trade carried on within; some, by means of a couple of "new-laid " eggs, as many loaves, and samples of sweetstuff; others by a tailor's card portraying the latest thing in coats and trousers ; or a brass plate on door indicates the abode of a dressmaker capable of designing the " latest fashion" in costumes or Court dresses; the main characteristic throughout being that everything that can possibly be discoloured or mildewed, is so.

Lodgings for single men abound; ladies apparently being not desirable. Strong odours, compounded of boiled greens, fried onions, bloaters, and toasted bacon, mingled with whiffs of old clothing, dustbins, and family washing, are invariable concomitants of these streets.

Shabby and forlorn hens and dried-up ducks shuffle about in the gutter, ever trending towards the greengrocer's shop, outside where they pretend they are in the country. Dirty children sit and play on the door-steps, share the gutter with the ducks and fowls, or tear about the roadway, yelled at by frowsy mothers, who, bare-armed and buttonless, stand at the doors and discuss local affairs with their neighbours, or bargain with the costermongers, who at all hours of the day shout mackerel, cauliflowers, watercress, radishes and celery, paraffin-oil, firewood, clothes-props, etc., impartially, or chaff the coal-retailers or the milkmen who never fail in their daily and indispensable rounds.

A great many of these streets are, like those described by Dickens, faded and tumble-down, with two irregular rows of tall meagre houses generally let out into lodgings where all kinds of small trades are plied, mostly by foreigners. The doors of these tenements are seldom closed, and a row of much-used bells denoting the various floors, suggest that the lodgers wait upon themselves. The shops in the neighbourhood cater chiefly for French and Germans, and remind one of the poorer quarters of Paris or Frankfort. There are Gallic restaurants, and Teutonic restaurations, where dinners a la carte or a prix fixe can be had of fair quality and at astonishingly low prices; besides which, there are the usual London eating-houses and coffee-shops where plates of meat at threepence, coffee at a halfpenny a cup, and halfpenny slices of pudding are largely sold. Round about are boucheries, where carcasses are cut up into strange-looking joints that yet seem handier and less wasteful than those we are more familiar with; charcuteries, prettily decked out, where, besides pork, are displayed in tempting array, pates, galantines, pressed-beef, croquettes, etc., and every imaginable kind of sausage; boulangeries, in whose windows are the familiar long white loaves side by side with brown ones, and the Westphalian "pimpernickel." Then one comes across crockery-shops, with the coarse but serviceable brown ware so much used in France, coffee-pots, pots-au-feu, jars, and the like. Blanchisseuses display linen got up a merveille. Modistes, chaussetiers and bottiers tempt the weaker sex with prettily-arranged and well-made costumes, hosiery, and dainty boots and shoes. Here, too, can be found some of the very few places where can be bought the oval wooden boxes with black tops in which hats and bonnets are conveyed to and from the milliners.

The overcrowding of the Metropolis is perhaps the most pressing social problem of the day, and the most difficult to cope with. The poorer classes must live near their place of employment, being unable to afford even the smallest and cheapest railway-fare; while the value of land anywhere near the centres of business is so great, and the demolition of small houses thereon to make room for big warehouses so continuous, that the filthiest and most meagre lodgings are filled to overflowing, though let for rents that absorb nearly all the scanty earnings of the tenants.

Overcrowding is also due to the fact, that whereas the increase or population is estimated at from fifty to sixty thousand per annum, the number of new tenements is comparatively small, or, at any rate, disproportionate. For example, in Kensington, one of the wealthiest parishes in the world, one quarter of the population live two or more persons in a room. In Soho, ten per cent. live, on an average, four to one apartment. In Whitechapel, the average is ten to a room—a density of about 225 persons to each acre. In Spitalfields, 4575 houses are let out in single rooms, of which 1400 are occupied by four to eleven persons each.

Distinct from the "regular-wage" earning community, there is an immense class in London, whose earnings are entirely precarious, some being, in unfavourable weather, cut off altogether.

First and foremost of these is the hard-working costermonger (under which denomination I include hawkers and stall-keepers), familiarized to West-enders by the clever impersonations of Mr. Albert Chevalier. Whether the name is, or is not, derived from the vending of "costards," a species of apple, is uncertain, but the "coster" has existed for centuries and was a familiar figure in the streets of Plantagenet and Tudor London.

The stock-in-trade of the present-day coster is contained in a barrow, owned or hired, to which he is sometimes able to harness a donkey; but when he attains this height of prosperity, he, as a rule, calls himself a "general dealer." Probably all costers at one time carried their goods in baskets, but the modern costermonger rather looks down on his comrade, the hawker, who has neither barrow nor truck. At night, the well-to-do coster, converting his barrow into a stall, lights it up with naphtha, the poorer one having to be content with the humble candle, as in the earlier times. Besides fruit and the commoner vegetables, all kinds of cheap foreign fruit and tomatoes are sold by them, and, in their season, mackerel, herrings, cauliflowers, asparagus, melons, strawberries, cherries, holly, cut flowers, and growing plants. Costers, as a class, have made much progress of late years. Their name used to be a term of contempt, and the bearers of it noted for roughness, but the efforts of Lord Shaftesbury and others on their behalf, have worked a wondrous improvement in their language and ways.

Amongst women, the most hardly-earned wages are those of tailoresses. Other occupations for women—somewhat better paid—are the shelling of walnuts and peas on the confines of fruit and vegetable markets, paper-bag-making; sack-making; fur-pulling, choking to the lungs and blinding to the eyes; and the raking-over of refuse heaps in dust-yards, sorting out bits of string, flannel, cardboard, and rag, anything in fact that can be converted into paper or shoddy cloth. But the most disgusting occupation for females, though not so uncertain, is the preparation of animal entrails for manufacture into sausage-skins; the greasy, slimy lengths of intestines are scraped until denuded of fat, etc., then turned inside out and thoroughly cleansed, again washed, and finally twisted up and dressed with salt for the market, the stench of the operation being nauseating.

Curiously-earned livelihoods are endless in variety: among them, that of the maker and vendor of fly-papers, with his cry of "Catch 'em alive, blue-bottles and flies." Then there are the miscellaneous vocations (of which one man may be engaged in several), such as "calling" people early in the morning, achieved by tapping at the windows with a rod until the sleeper wakes; oiling people's gates for a halfpenny a time; picking up the scattered oats, chopped hay, etc., found lying about cab-stands, and selling it to cabmen at a very cheap rate.

A few collect newspaper-contents-bills, and sell a quantity for a halfpenny to unfortunate sleepers-out, who use them as a protection from the damp air and cold flags. Then there are cab-runners —men who run after luggage-laden cabs to earn a copper by carrying the luggage into the house; and "cab-glimmers," who open and shut cab-doors, and with their hand protect the lady's dress from the wheel as she gets in and out of the cab. The collecting of cigar-ends is another industry of the streets; these are sold to florists at from 6d. to 10d. per pound to fumigate plants with.

Pavement-artists make ,but an uncertain living at best, though now and again they make a "haul" when some enthusiastic passer-by is impressed by their "latent talent." Many of these men do really draw the productions announced as " All the work of my own hand," but others get an expert to execute the pictures, pay for them, and pass them off as their own."

Chapter 5: The Countryside

Due to various governmental changes since the 1970s, the map of England today looks somewhat different from its Edwardian counterpart. Some counties have disappeared, some have decreased in size, and some have been invented from large metropolitan areas. Nevertheless, the basic character of the countryside remains despite—or perhaps in spite of—the myriad of ways people, technology, and warfare has affected it.

These shires—which could be very loosely defined as "states"—were created as administrative areas, which is why so many older peerages are named for a particular county (*e.g.,* Duke of Devonshire) or why courtesy titles (which are usually the original peerage from which an ancestor was raised to a higher rank) are named after towns or cities that the newly-ennobled influenced. But this chapter is not about the peerage and its rules and complexities.

Life in the Edwardian Countryside
The English have always loved their countryside, and as stated before, roots in the country were of vital importance: it represented—literally—the strength, the wealth, and the political might of the elite. During the Edwardian era, the countryside ironically witnessed the exodus of underemployed and largely impoverished workers and farmers for factories in cities and the influx of artists, poets, and the well-to-do inspired by its beauty and simplicity.

The agricultural depression of the last twenty years of the 19th century had hit the land and its workers hard, but those that had survived setbacks reaped the benefits of the land's recovery. Yet, despite the technological advances and the "rural exodus" of laborers and workers, old village customs and traditions experienced a brief resurgence of popularity, no doubt fueled by the uneasy aristocrats and artists who felt the decline of land meant the decline of Britannia. Over the day, I will detail life in the countryside for the social elite, the farmers, and the artists who lived, worked, and played in a world whose end was signaled by WWI.

Edwardian farmers reaped the benefits of a newly-recovered economy. Though some skepticism of better times remained, on the whole, freeholders and tenant farmers alike had a good prospect of making a profit from their labors. Their optimism was characterized in the increasing adoption of new and expensive farming technologies like steam operated equipment, seed drills, threshing machines, and tractors.

Into the market also came fancy artificial fertilizers and feedstuffs for livestock. Another addition was the new generation of farmer, some of whom had little to no experience in agriculture, who had a fresher view of the situation. They, combined with the new innovations and improvements, took Edwardian farming to a new level.

Most farmers of the period had what was known as a "mixed farm"—land allotted for crops and land allotted for livestock. They grew wheat, barley, root crops, and hay ("cereals"), on the former, and raised cattle and sheep on the latter. Few farmers devoted themselves to one crop, or to one animal, though some farms in the Fens were known for their excellent potatoes.

Most farms were of a modest scale, with more than half if the 340,000 farms of more than five acres being smaller than fifty acres, and only 37% between fifty and three hundred acres in size. 90% of the farmers working the land were tenant farmers—that is, they rented their farms from great landowners and paid the rents from what they earned from the sale of their produce and livestock.

A typical farm was managed by the family, with employees ranging from carters to shepherds to day laborers—many of them relatives. Unlike their predecessors, Edwardian farmers were likely to be educated, having benefited from the 1870 educational act and the founding of colleges for agriculture.

Our Edwardian farmer now had technical know-how of soils, animals, and crops, and could use these skills to solve problems on the farm that his father or grandfather before him would have left to fate.

The beginning of the agricultural year was October 11, or "Old Michaelmas". The farm was plowed to break up the cereal harvest and prepared for the sowing of winter corn. After this was the task of clearing ditches, trimming hedges, and cutting the first of the roots, which would last into January. This was followed by the cultivating, rolling, and harrowing for the spring. Hay was farmed in the summer, and plowing the summer fallow took place. Throughout this, the cattle and sheep were prepared for their destination, though the prices of wool had fallen in the Victorian era and had yet to fully recover.

Since most farmers were, as stated before, tenant farmers, they took ample part in the festivities and entertainments of the local area. Most villages possessed a cricket green, there were various societies got up by citizens—the most popular being theatrical societies—, and no one needed an excuse for a county ball or dance. Also, like in other areas of Edwardian society, farmers began to organize into trade unions, which influenced the political persuasions of Parliamentary candidates.

However, prosperity for farmers did not automatically equal prosperity for the great landowners. During the agricultural depression, many landowners lowered the rents or extended longer grace periods for their tenants, thereby decreasing their annual profits. As a result, many were forced to sell large tracts of their land to speculators and would-be landowners. The decline in number of rural laborers, both skilled and unskilled, made finding new tenants difficult, and it grew increasingly common for whole estates to be leased or sold to *nouveaux riches* who fancied playing "Squire" and turned good farmland into shooting or hunting territory.

Though the agricultural depression lifted during the early years of Edward VII's reign, but the well-to-do did not cease their country pursuits, and the Edwardian era was also the last hurrah of the great country house party. The birth of the motorcar—and creation of roads on which to drive—revitalized the inns and shops virtually abandoned once the railway made travel cheap, fast, and easy.

Once more, irony via new technology rears its head: the very technological advances that made work in the city attractive to the children of farmers also made the country attractive to the social elite. Society periodicals of the mid-Edwardian era lamented to sharp decrease in number of those taking part in the Season once everyone adopted the motorcar, as many chose to motor between country houses and Town during the months were it was previously de rigueur to live in London. This mobility brought about the creation of the automobile tour. Armed with a luncheon hamper, a spare tire, and a map, motorists would set off on a drive around a particular section of the countryside, visiting sites and architecture that had mostly fallen into obscurity (villagers were frequently perplexed by the excitement an old Roman ruin aroused in these visitors).

Very soon, bookstores abounded with travelogues and handbooks detailing the hows, whens, and whats of motor touring, and it became the craze to jump into one's automobile and drive to the remotest areas of the earth. This lead to the long-held notion that the automobile was a rich man's plaything and that motoring was a sport (cheaper cars, which were available to the middle classes, democratized the motorcar, but kept the sport accessible only to the rich).

Others who found inspiration in obscure Roman ruins, verdant pastures, and wildlife were artists, poets, and writers. One particular movement had a "back to our roots" zeitgeist—the Arts & Crafts Movement, which was a reaction against the artificial, the imitation, and the gaudiness born from the Industrial Revolution.

William Morris was the founder of this movement, and "students" of his ideas, such as garden designer Gertrude Jekyll, architect Edwin Lutyens, and designer Charles Rennie Mackintosh, went on to create interiors and exteriors that were shocking to most of Edwardian society.

Proponents of Arts & Crafts considered proportion, space, simplicity, and harmony more important than displaying one's wealth through crowded rooms, heavy imitation furniture, and neo-Gothic mansions. They also valued England's historic craftsmanship, and held exhibitions to display typesetting, embroidery, and other decorative arts that had been superseded by machines rather than hands. The movement had also spread to Ireland and Scotland, and in the former, was an impetus to preserving Irish culture and crafts.

Life in the Edwardian countryside presented another of those dichotomies so characteristic of the era. As the elite and well-to-do fought to maintain and revive old arts, pastimes, and customs (and in the case of Ireland, used them to strengthen nationalist movements), the rural population rejected their traditional place in society. They not only desired a better life, but were avid adopters of the technology the Arts & Crafts movement abhorred. Far from viewing the countryside with the starry-eyed romanticism of artists, farmers and villagers and craftsmen and women now viewed their work as earning them the right to own their land and to have a voice in politics, and soon society was forced to oblige.

Major Cities

London was the heart of Britain and the Empire, but there were many other major cities who played a definite role in Edwardian society. We shall focus on Manchester in particular, which in itself was the heart of northern England, England's industries, and its political agitations.

This city's importance is noticeable in its presence in two major period dramas: Gaskell's North and South, and Downton Abbey. Manchester, more than any other city in

England, characterized the shift in power from the traditional landed gentry and aristocracy to the might of industry. The growth of Manchester from a northern market town into an industrial and financial powerhouse was rather like the transformation of New York from Dutch village to five boroughs.

As the hub of the Industrial Revolution, the primary industry was cotton. Cotton was transported from Liverpool to the mills, and from these mills sprang bleach works, textile design firms, and foundries. So important to the industry was Manchester and the surrounding area, it was soon dubbed "Cottonopolis." The rapid growth of the city was helped by advances in transportation—river navigation, railways, and omnibus services—and the multitude of people moving to Manchester for work.

Manchester was also the natural hub for radicalism and reform, and the Manchester Guardian soon carved out a place in the nation's papers for its hard-line stance against the status quo. By the Edwardian era, Manchester was one of the largest regions in the world, and its industry had expanded to engineering and chemical fields. Yet, despite all of this growth and prosperity, Manchester's citizens did not escape crippling poverty. The city had its slums and crime and despair just like London, and for all the rags-to-riches industrialists running factories and mills, marginalization and income disparity was even more acute amongst workers.

However, these workers were more vituperative than in London, and the 1890s witnessed the birth of the Labour Party. There were pockets of Conservative strongholds in the Edwardian era, but during the election of 1906, old-time MPs soon realized no seats were safe from social revolution.

Other important English cities of the Edwardian era were:

- Liverpool, the principle seaport of England, which burst into importance when the sea link between it and America was established in the 1840s. Manufactured items were exported—cotton from Manchester, and coal from Wales—and American raw cotton, grain, and

breadstuffs, Irish cattle and butter, and Canadian timber were imported.
• Folkestone, a thriving and fashionable seaside resort on the southern coast.
• Blackpool, a seaside resort in Lancashire geared towards the working class and factory workers.
• Bristol, a very important trading town. Manufactured of chocolate, soap, leather, and glass. Later a hob of British aviation.
• Birmingham, the chief center of England and the most important industrial town after Manchester.
• Coventry, major city in the West Midlands and center of bicycle and motorcar manufacturing.
• Sheffield, another principal manufacturing town known for its cutlery, steel, and iron goods.

Chapter 6: Amusements and Entertainments

Sports
During the Victorian and Edwardian eras, sports became serious business. There was the tug-of-war between professionals and amateurs, the agenda of sports in boys' and girls' public schools, new fads that swept the nation, the reemergence of the Olympic Games, and the participation of women.

The theory of "Muscular Christianity," wherein physical activity and health were merged with morality, which in turn was credited for the might of British imperialism was the primary influence upon the era—and could be pinpointed as one of the forces which lead countless young men to rush off to war in 1914. Nevertheless, during the early twentieth century, sport had become commonplace in everyone's lives, so commonplace in fact, that those who did not participate were looked upon as oddities.

The "downside," so to speak, for the ubiquitous of sports, was that men and women from lower classes became just as proficient as those who honed their skills in public school or at house parties. They met the demands for public sporting events and tournaments, but because they were not well off, they expected to be paid for their talents. This schism between well-to-do "amateur" sportsmen and "professional" sportsmen was most prominent in cricket and association football (soccer).

In earlier days, both played together on the same local teams, and the high profile matches were those played between Eton and Harrow, and Oxford and Cambridge, at the Lord's Cricket Oval in London. You would be right to assume that these events became yet another fashionable segment of the London Season and was not very amenable to the rowdier elements.

The tide changed when Australia beat England four consecutive times during a Test Match tour—which until then, had been financed by private cricket clubs or benefactors—and the Metropolitan Cricket Club took responsibility for future test matches. Since every town and village had its cricket club, and colliers, churches, institutes, factories, and schools their own teams, there was a plethora of excellent cricket players to fill these major cricket clubs.

The same happened with association football, and it is in the 1880s when the major football clubs still in existence today were formed. Professionalism was legalized in 1885, but the disparities in wealth between the clubs lead to poaching of good players from poor clubs, and a law was passed in 1901 by the F.A. that no player could be signed for more than £10 and paid no more than £208 a year, before bonuses dependent upon the outcome of a match.

As stated above, the English public school was heart of sporting life. From the moment boys of 12 or 13 entered Winchester or Eton, they were expected to prove their ability on the cricket fields, at football, rowing, tennis, and a host of games indigenous to the school. The boy who did not play sports would find it difficult to make friends because everyone was so focused on physical prowess, he would be left out of the cultural fabric of the school.

There was also the notion that if boys spent their waking hours playing and studying, there would be no time or inclination for immorality. This line of reasoning tipped the scales in support of sports at girls' schools in the 1870s, when commonly held beliefs warned that excessive physical activity would ruin female reproductive organs and would make them masculine. Many headmistresses still struggled with allowing their girls to play sports up until the 1890s, but cultural forces of the decade toppled that reluctance.

Overall, sport rapidly infiltrated every element of society. First was the craze for bicycles. They were very popular in France in the 1880s, and this spread to England by the latter half of the decade. In the 1890s, bicycles declined in price, and the bicycle tour became a common sight in the English countryside. The bicycle also broke down the system of chaperonage that kept unmarried young ladies away from unmarried young men. After all, it would be difficult for a mother or elderly chaperone to keep up with a group of furiously pedaling ladies and gentlemen!

Other crazes included tennis (lawn and court), which also gave rise to professional tournaments, and golf, which had come down from Scotland in the 1860s and grew in popularity after Prime Minister Balfour, a Scot who detested traditional sports like shooting and fox hunting, spent his leisure hours on the green. There was also jiu-jitsu, popularized by the Japanese athletes brought over during the brief bartitsu fad, table tennis/ping-pong, and billiards.

Of those traditional sports, fox hunting and shooting were the province only of the wealthy. For one thing, both required land, specialized staff, and expensive animals. Fox hunting also required money to keep up the Hunt, and many a bankrupt Hunt Master was forced to sell his entire stable and kennel to someone who could afford to run the hunt. Hunting could also be exclusive, and the best hunting areas were in Melton Mowbray—famous for its Stilton cheese and pork pies—and in Ireland.

Shooting—pheasant, grouse, partridge, woodcock, snipe, or even big game in Africa or Asia—was the sport of excess. Edward VII and his son George V were the big guns of the era, and thousands of birds were shot down at individual shooting parties. So excessive were these events, even George V was to admit the sport had gone too far when during one party, nearly 10,000 partridges had been felled by the guns.

Though it was rare for women to take part in the higher profile sports such as cricket or shooting, they were present in just about every other sport available. In girls' schools, students were mad for basketball and field hockey, and when older, they rode horses, sailed small yachts or catboats, swam, drove four-in-hands, punted along the Thames, stalked deer in Scotland, played the aforementioned golf and tennis, and later, drove and raced motorcars and flew airplanes.

This was the age of the Sportswoman, and publishers of books and periodicals quickly flooded the market with guides, magazines, articles, and newspaper columns on how to play these sports. New magazines like the *Ladies' Field* sat beside traditional male sports' periodicals like *The Sporting Times*, and even the most traditional ladies' magazines like the *Queen* and *The Lady* bowed to the trend and added regular columns written by imminent sportswomen.

The emphasis on sports contributed to the reemergence of the Olympic Games in 1896. Held in Athens as a nod to the last Olympic Games in 776, the ten days were devoted to fencing, weightlifting, gymnastics, tennis, shooting, marathons, cycling, and yachting. Like today, it was a time of solidarity and competition, and by the dawn of WWI, the world witnessed six Olympic meetings in St Louis, Stockholm, London, Paris, and Athens.

Sports during the Edwardian era could both unite and divide, but at best, it leveled the playing field—no pun intended—for the disadvantaged. It also promoted discipline and brother/sisterhood, and it's for no reason the Duke of Wellington was said to proclaim the battle of Waterloo was won on the playing fields of Eton. Yet, this devotion to sports, and what it stood for, possessed shades of gray, not simply because of its influence upon young men during WWI, but for its role in the colonization of the world.

Amusements and Entertainments
When in 1914, Eliza Doolittle (played by Mrs. Patrick Campbell) uttered the word "Bloody" on stage, it aroused gasps of outrage, but there were no cries for the Lord Chamberlain to shut it down, and night after night, audiences

packed the house even more firmly. By then, primed by the lavish revues of the music hall and musical comedy, the decadence of the Ballet Russes, the pomp of Beerbohm Tree's and Ellen Terry's interpretations of Shakespeare, the lightly witty plays of J.M. Barrie, and the "rough" social plays of Shaw, Ibsen, and Maugham, audiences had long come to expect shock and spectacle.

The tide had turned in 1903, when the new Gaiety Theatre reopened after its demolition and relocation during improvements to the Strand. The old Gaiety had been an antiquated hall, but now, under the aegis of George Edwardes, it was the home of frothy and fantastic musical comedy, underpinned by the delectable row of chorus girls known as "Gaiety Girls." One by one, they were snatched up by the crème of the aristocracy, and Denise Orme, Sylvia Storey, and Olive May, were soon transformed into the Baroness Churston, the Countess Poulett, and the Countess of Drogheda.

Light opera made stars of Gabrielle Ray, Zena Dare, and Lily Elsie, the last of whom was pushed into the stratosphere when she starred in The Merry Widow, which ran from June 1907 to July 1909. Edward VII saw it four times, and when it made its final bow, audiences besieged the Gaiety all day long, with some staking out their place in line as early as 5:30 AM.

The music hall, which had grown a bit creaky and suspect in the last decade of the nineteenth century, was revived in huge, gorgeously decorated theatres like the Alhambra and the Coliseum. Stars could earn more than £1000 a week, and venerable actresses like Sarah Bernhardt and Ellen Terry raked in money performing one-act plays as part of the general program.

Tease and titillation became part of the music hall: Gaby Deslys made her name singing naughty French songs, Maud Allan bared her arms and legs in her infamous role as Salome, and Australian swimmer Annette Kellerman did a swimming and diving act in skin-tight bathing costume. Male impersonators were also very popular, and Vesta Tilley was so adored, she set men's fashions.

There was a brief lull around the early 1910s, when musical comedies and halls had stagnated, but the transition of Victorian burlesque into the modern revue with *Hullo, Ragtime!* in 1912 and *Hullo, Tango!* in 1913 brought it back into vogue. As evident by their names, these two revues tapped into the craze for ragtime and its dances.

Serious theatre was found at the Haymarket, St. James's, and Drury Lane. All had the approval of royalty, and also possessed a venerable reputation for quality plays performed by quality actors. Henry Irving, the Victorian era's greatest dramatic actor, died in 1901, and the mantle was quickly assumed by Beerbohm Tree, who ran His Majesty's Theatre. Tree's staging of Shakespeare became legendary, and his affordable seats, free programs, and no cloakroom charges made him popular with theatre goers from all tiers of society.

The brightest star during the Edwardian era was J.M. Barrie. His whimsical and warm-hearted plays brought cheer to every viewer, and oddly enough, Beerbohm Tree thought Barrie was mad when he read Peter Pan in 1904. Fortunately, American impresario Charles Frohman disagreed, and staged the play to great success at the Duke of York's, and later in America with the popular actress, Maude Adams.

The theatre allowed one to escape for a few hours, but Edwardians could also physically escape to the various seaside resorts along England's coast. The aristocracy preferred the French Riviera or Edward VII's favorite destination, Biarritz, but Brighton, Lyme Regis, Scarborough, or Margate were just as good—if not better, in the minds of more xenophobic—for upper and middle class Britons.

Clare Leighton was born to two authors, and described the family's annual exodus from their home in St. John's Wood to a summer home in East Anglia in her memoirs, *Tempestuous Petticoat:*

> "The migrations started a week or two before we actually took the journey by train, for there was so much to be packed. Countless linen chests and trunks appeared on our landings, and in odd corners of all the rooms....though the trunks stood waiting, there was one unpleasant ritual to perform before the packing could take place. My mother's furs must be put away for the summer. Her ermine stole and muff, her sable stole and her skunk-trimmed velvet coat must be protected in pepper from the ravages of moths....Once the furs were safely protected against moths, my mother was free to put her mind to the packing for the annual exodus....everything that lay about [her] study was tossed into these trunks...even my father's easel and painting materials had to be strapped together and packed. The only thing of importance we did not take was the gramophone.
>
> It was a good-sized gathering when it assembled for the migration. First there were the heads of the tribe, my father and mother...then of course, there were we three children. Walmy [Mrs. Walmisley, Mrs. Leighton's secretary]...And then came the staff, the nurse and undernurse."

The Leightons initially rented a furnished home in Lowestoft, but later purchased a home overlooking the North Sea. Their stay during the summer months was mimicked by countless families, and for the most part, seaside resorts rarely varied in appearance. All had promenades stretching to the beach, a stand for bands and minstrel players, bathing huts where one changed into bathing costume, open-air restaurants, and cricket grounds.

In Scotland, cricket grounds were exchanged for golf links, though many in England did offer this option. These summer excursions were not limited to the well-to-do. In fact, the growth of the railway was fostered by lines heading straight to seaside resorts (many hotels were owned by the railway companies), and third class tickets could take a factory worker or mill hand to Blackpool, or Southport, or Redcar with ease. In fact, so profitable were seaside resorts, Lord De La Warr created his own resort in Kent (Bexhill-on-Sea), and the directorships of many hotel and resort syndicates boasted illustrious names.

For the more adventurous, it was just as easy and inexpensive to get away from England. Thomas Cook & Son so perfected the art of travel, one could stay in a little oasis of "England" whether you were in Cairo or Constantinople. This, plus the combination of Baedeker or Murray guidebook, cheap railway fare, and fast "ocean greyhounds", enabled the English to experience foreign travel at a premium.

Depending on income, Edwardian travelers had the choice of lavish hotel, respectable boarding house or pensione, or rented house or villa. Servants were cheap and plentiful, and food was good (guidebooks like Baedeker were meticulous in their recommendation of good restaurants and eateries). In fact, so cosseted were English travelers, it was rare to experience any difficulties or surprises over the course of their journey.

The social elite tended to follow in the King's footsteps: Biarritz, Carlsbad or Marienbad, and Paris, or foreign courts (Berlin, St. Petersburg, Rome). Florence and Venice were most popular with artists and Cairo with those interested in antiquities or recovering their health, while the more adventurous went to Bombay or Peking. Sporting tours were highly popular with men—tiger shoots in India, moose hunting in America, or Big Game in Africa—where one's prowess was tied to the size of the prize.

To return to domestic entertainments, the most enduring focused on music and art. Music accompanied almost every pastime, whether it be a dance, a musicale, or merely a pint in a pub. Opera singers of the time, such as Nellie Melba and Enrico Caruso, were treated like deities, and could command exorbitant sums for private performances. Musical accomplishments were also encouraged in both young men and women, though for the latter more so than the former, and marriage-minded mamas knew the reaction of men to the alabaster arms of their daughters as they played a piano solo at an At Home performance.

The middle classes formed musical societies, where they revived ancient instruments like the lyre, or even adopted newfangled ones like the ukulele. In the days before the radio, the only way to hear the latest tunes, usually from the stage, were on sheet or the gramophone, and soon every well-to-do home had its own record player.

Sport and amusements were important to every segment of society, though naturally some had more opportunity than experience than others. Yet each played a significant role in shaping and influencing both groups and individuals.

Chapter 7: Behind Closed Doors

The Family
The concept of "family" in English society is rooted in centuries of tradition. Whereas in America, individualism rules—even during the 1900s—it was the complete opposite across the Atlantic. From the bottom of society all the way to the top, the goals, desires, and aims of a person were largely geared towards fulfilling family prerogatives and expectations. At the top was the paterfamilias—the father.

The focus will remain on the aristocracy, and the fictional 8th Marquess of Blankshire a stand-in. Lord Marquess married to Lady Blankshire, and had six children--four sons and two daughters. From birth, the 8th Marquess was raised with the expectation of ruling his home (Blankshire Manor), his land, his tenants, the livings (rector or parish priest), and, to a lesser extent than in the past, the parliamentary seats in his area.

The upbringing of his eldest son, the Earl of Blank, was the same. As such, Lord Blankshire was "father" to his bloodline and to his underlings, and took a rather paternalistic view of people. In the countryside, this was respected, and as he met or passed his tenants and villagers, they never fail to doff their caps and murmur "Your lordship" (the type of behavior the urban working classes bucked against).

Marriages in the upper and aristocratic classes were generally based on affection, and sometimes even love, but the structure and insularity of the family within society made sure a man and woman felt affection for or fell in love with the right person! Lady Blankshire brought a dowry and family connections to her marriage to Lord Blankshire, and giving birth to six children not only fulfilled the purpose of marriage, but also established another generation from which to strengthen and build alliances and wealth.

Sons were preferred because they brought wealth into the family, but a daughter could make an excellent match and raise the family fortune and/or status (for example, Lord Elcho [later Lord Wemyss] had three daughters—Cynthia, Mary, and Irene. Cynthia and Mary made love matches with upper class suitors, but Irene was pushed into an excellent match with a peer, and on the strength of that, Irene received the largest dowry of the sisters).

Lady Blankshire, as with all upper class women, was supposed to provide the moral foundation of the family and of the estate, and the behavior and prosperity of the children, the servants, and the tenants were supposed to reflect her rule. As the moral foundation, she took a hand in county matters, from the establishment of schools and hospitals, the running of charities, to the health of tenants.

The colloquial term for all of this was "Lady Bountiful," and Lady Blankshire and her daughters took their position quite seriously. The running of Blankshire Manor was of the utmost importance, and a primary reason why young American heiress brides found life in England so uncomfortable was due to their ignorance of how to run a great establishment. When the servants knew you had no clue how to direct them, they lost respect for their mistress and havoc was wreaked in the subtlest manner known only by servants.

The younger sons of the Blankshires were, to be blunt, left to make their own way in life as primogeniture meant that the estate, the land, the income from the land, and the title, went only to their eldest brother. They received an allowance, as did their sisters, but they could not afford to set up their own household and raise a family on that small sum. The traditional fields for younger sons were the army, the House of Commons, and the church because they were another extension of the power exercised by the ruling elite.

However, the rising costs of living (in particular the church, whose salaries declined greatly, and the army, where, in the smartest regiments, one was required to own a string of polo ponies, purchase the spiffiest uniforms, belong to the right clubs, and pay for the expensive mess bills!) meant the younger sons needed to obtain a lucrative position.

The expansion of the Empire saw the creation of the civil service, though this soon became competitive when the rising middle classes—educated at the good, but not elite public and grammar schools—clamored for entry, turning the ruling of the Empire into a bit of a meritocracy.

However, a good marriage to a wealthy woman would do much for one's bank account and one's career—especially in politics, where a wife was expected to help and push her husband into prominence. Woe betide the politician who married an awkward and ignorant girl incapable of shouldering her social duties. Nevertheless, the younger son was raised with the expectation of being yet another arm of his family's might and power, albeit on a slightly less grander scale than his titled brother.

The daughters of the Blankshires were raised to be wives. As seen in the chapter about the London Season, she was groomed to be the wife of a particular type of man and if the sons were considered an extension of the mother's rule, the daughters definitely were even more so, and it took a girl of very strong will to defy her mother's wishes. Lady Evelyn Murray, the youngest daughter of the Duke of Atholl, was one such girl, and after refusing to take part in the Season—instead choosing to visit museums, read books, and attend lectures—her father packed her off to Europe with an allowance and a companion.

In the same way, if a mother did not want her daughters to marry, she could make that happen: though the public adored Queen Alexandra as all that was kind and good, in private she held firmly to her daughters as playmates and servants. Queen Victoria was upset about this, and advised her son, the then Prince of Wales, to push Alix out of this mindset, but the then Princess of Wales turned a deaf ear—literally—to his hints.

Ultimately, the two eldest daughters—Louise and Maud—managed to marry, but Princess Victoria was kept as her mother's companion, single and forever at beck and call, until Alix died in 1925.

When someone stepped out of line, the entire family closed rank to put pressure of them until they were pressed back into conformity. If this did not work, the family member was, as with Lady Evelyn, sent away with an allowance to live in obscurity. The official term was "Remittance Man" and the spread of the Empire created all sorts of nooks and crannies into which an errant son or daughter or cousin could be chucked.

This pressure could not really be placed on the head of the family, but they could try, as seen in the case of the "Dancing" Marquess of Anglesey, who was married to his cousin in, no doubt, an attempt to curb his scandalous ways and frittering away of his vast fortune. Unfortunately, his wife could not stick out his eccentricities and obtained a divorce after two years of marriage. The "Dancing Marquess" ended up dying in 1905, having run up a debt of £544,000 since inheriting his title. Overall, scandal and profligacy were averted or hushed up because the family unit was all and everything to the English. In addition, the family unit of the aristocracy was there to keep everything in order and in control.

The other side of the family was its size. Queen Victoria did set the public ideal for a large family, but by the late Victorian and Edwardian eras, ladies grew a bit more bold about limiting their pregnancies. Gynecological texts and books for "married women only" published in the mid-19th century provide information on family planning, but technology had to catch up with this albeit taboo subject. Though rubber condoms were available, they were mostly used for the prevention of disease from prostitutes--not to prevent pregnancy--so couples relied upon more primitive methods, such as withdrawal, to minimize the chances of pregnancy

According to Pamela Horn's *High Society*, "it has been estimated that of those landed aristocrats who married in the 1830s an average of about 7 births per fertile couple was recorded. By the 1870s this had fallen to between 4 and 5 births to each marriage, and in the 1880s to just over 3, with the trend continuing down, to average between 2 and 3 births per marriage on the eve of WWI."

This decrease in children seems to have coincided with the agricultural depression which pushed income from the land way down (hence the need for the heiress bride), as well as the increase in the educated middle and lower classes who could compete with the upper classes and aristocracy for position and occupation. However, young ladies still went to the marriage bed mostly innocent and ignorant of the mechanics of sex, pregnancy, and contraception, and only few dared to find pleasure in sexual relations and to limit their childbearing by contraceptive means.

The Edwardian Home
The Edwardian home differed little from the Victorian home, save that of decoration and purpose. Where the Victorians filled their homes to the brim with knickknacks, chair and sofa coverings, heavy furniture, plants, and carpets, the Edwardians gradually began to adopt the streamlined and open-air aesthetics preached by those in the Arts & Crafts movement. Granted, most aristocrats continued to live alongside the clutter and antiques accumulated after centuries, but members of The Souls, a clique made up of the aristocratic intelligentsia, were keen to move against the tide of their peers, and Percy and Madeleine Wyndham—the heart of the clique—commissioned Philip Webb to Clouds House in Wiltshire to fulfill these principles. But overall, aristocrats and the Americans who entered their world, preferred the lavish and the opulent, and had homes built or redecorated for this purpose.

The middle classes, newly "genteel", were prime targets for the manufacturers churning out imitation Jacobean or imitation Empire style furniture. Yet their homes served a much different function when compared to the wealthy and upper class, for they did not entertain on a huge scale, nor could they afford huge homes to house 10+ servants. As a result their homes were more utilitarian and less focused on public rooms, and they were also much more likely to live in houses with up-to-date appliances such as electric stoves or central heating, to make up for the lack of domestic staff. Lower down the scale, the housing of the working class and poor varied greatly, with some existing in cramped and poorly ventilated slums, some in cottages on country estates, and others in the newly-created housing estates built for the improvement of the poor.

The housing of the underclass was a leading topic for Edwardian reformers, and during the 1890s and 1900s, the Councils of England's major cities took steps towards providing homes for the working class. Birmingham, Leeds, Bradford, and Manchester took the lead in providing municipal flats, but any plans for widespread council housing was checked by political antipathy and developers' greed. Liverpool, which was one of the fastest cities in 1900, pursued an aggressive policy of expanding its boundaries.

Between 1895 and 1914, eight suburbs were swallowed to create Greater Liverpool, and a major program of building council flats quickly followed. Between 1905 and 1906, a thousand three-story tenements had been built at a rate matched only in Glasgow (Scotland). However, it was the London County Council that surpassed all other efforts, via their Architect's Department.

According to Charles Booth's survey of the London poor, a million out of 4.5 million lived in grossly inadequate housing. The inhabitants of slums faced poor sanitation, lighting, and space on top of neglected buildings inspectors considered hazardous. This doesn't even take into account the numbers of homeless families dependent whose meager earnings couldn't even pay for the type of cheap and shoddy lodging already mentioned. The first housing project of the LCC was to house sixty people just off Holborn. The following project was much larger—housing 418 people in Southwark—and by 1908 flats in housing blocks had been built on twelve estates and housed 17,000 people.

To give an example of the transformation of a slum into a housing estate, here is a Before and After map of the notorious London slum, the Old Nichol, which was cleared and redeveloped in the late 1890s.

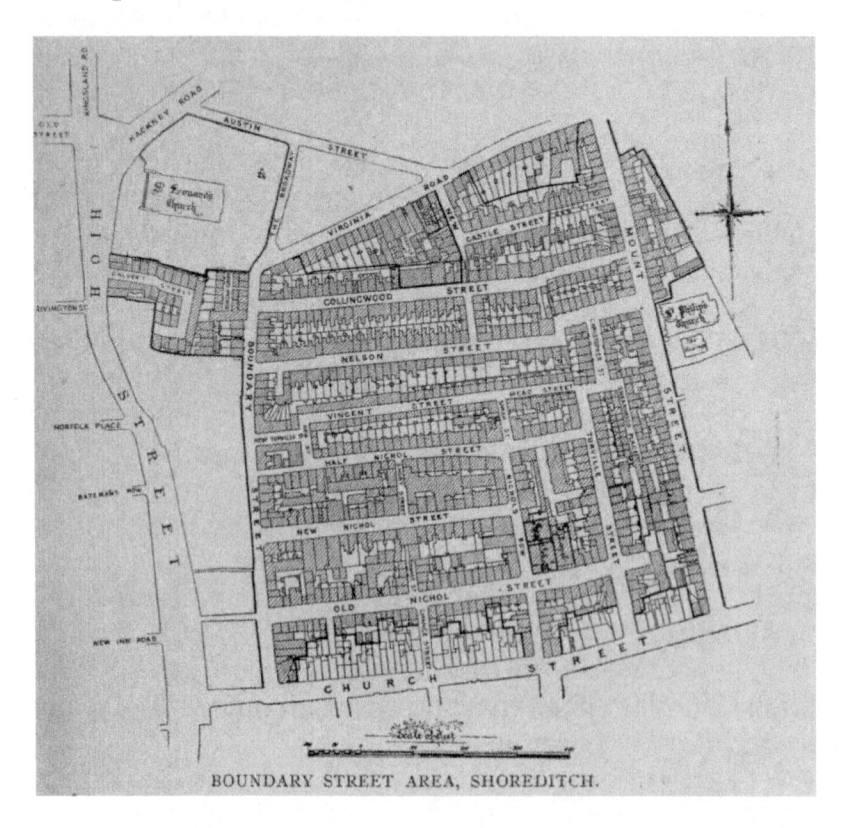

BOUNDARY STREET AREA, SHOREDITCH.

BOUNDARY STREET AREA AS RE-DEVELOPED.

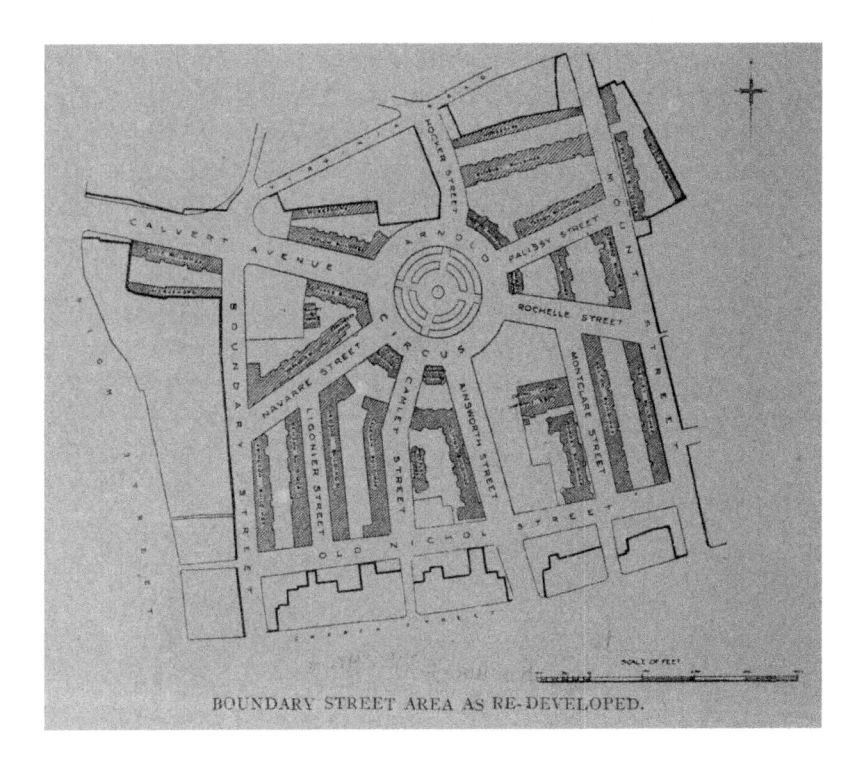

In their zeal for housing reform, the LCC cleared slums but also displaced tens of thousands of Londoners who had nowhere to go when evicted.
According to George Sims:
> "When a slum has been levelled to the ground a huge block of working class dwellings generally rises on its site. These buildings are wanted. Many of them are excellent. But up to the present they have hardly succeeded in solving the great problem, because the evicted or displaced tenants, practically left without any superior accommodation, are driven into worse.
> An ounce of practical experience is worth a ton of argument. Let us see for ourselves how an eviction works. Here is a grand new block of working class dwellings in Southwark. On the site where the building stands there stood a short while ago a network of courts and alleys inhabited mainly by poor people earning a precarious livelihood. After notice had been served

upon them some began at once to look about for other accommodation. But the larger number, because it is the nature of the slum dwellers to live only for to-day and to trust to luck for to-morrow, did nothing.

At last came the pinch. The authorities served the last notice, "Get out, or your walls will crumble about you." The tenant who after that still remained obstinate soon realised that the end had come. The roof, the doors, and the windows were removed while she (it is generally a woman) still remained crouching in a corner of the miserable room which contained the chair, the table, the bed, the frying pan, and the tub that were her 'furniture.'

Eventually the position became dangerous. When bricks and plaster began to fall in showers about her, and the point of the pickaxe came through the wall against which she was leaning, then at last she scrambled for her belongings and went out into the street, where a little crowd of onlookers and fellow sufferers welcomed her sympathetically.

Sometimes a whole family, the head having failed or neglected during the period of grace to find accommodation elsewhere, is turned into the street. I have seen families sitting homeless on their goods, which were piled high in the court. Guarding their household gods sat women with infants in their arms. They sat on, hopeless and despairing, and saw their homes demolished before their eyes.

Now and again the heap of bedding and furniture was diminished. A man would return and tell his wife he had found a place. They would gather up their goods and go. But all were not so fortunate. I have seen a woman with a child in her arms and two children crouching by her side sitting out long after nightfall by her flung-out furniture, because the husband could find no accommodation at the rent he could afford."

Despite these unfortunate circumstances, the council flats were clean, bright, airy, and were fitted up with up-to-date appliances. In fact, not only new houses and council estates possessed the latest in fittings, but middle-class villas, elegant apartment flats, and even the town houses and country estates owned by the well-to-do. Electricity was wired in the upstairs (some more conscientious masters had it wired belowstairs as well), new plumbing, telephones installed, and water closets added to the layout. The most opulent transformation occurred in the bathroom, where the wealthiest had their baths amongst heated town rails, metal holders fixed to the wall for tooth brushes, mirrors over the pedestal wash basins, tiled floors (white or blue were the vogue), frosted glass windows, and marble walls. Some even featured the newfangled needle shower.

The *Daily Mail* tapped into the zeitgeist for new and improved housing for the lower and middle classes and founded the Ideal Home Exhibition in 1908. The exhibition featured whole rooms in the latest styles, and dedicated entire sections to home life (kitchens, sitting rooms, etc). They even featured a competition to build the "ideal home", and the Arts and Crafts Movement featured heavily amongst all displays. This concerted effort to uplift the poor had its roots in the Victorian era, but by the turn of the century Socialists and reformers alike demanded more than mere charity bazaars and drumming up donations; they preferred action.

The Salvation Army, founded by William and Catherine Booth in 1865, combined militant charity with Christianity, and out of this was born the settlement movement. The most famous of these was Toynbee Hall, founded in 1884.

The aims of this movement were for the poor and rich to live together more closely. Situated in the poorer districts of London, middle and upper class volunteers lived in the settlement and ran programs providing food, shelter, and education for the poor amongst them. The first settlement homes were aligned with universities and a particular Anglican theology (High Church, Low Church), though later ones were founded by philanthropists (such as author Mrs. Humphry Ward, who founded the Passemore Edwards Settlement in

1898). The settlement movement was also a place for women to shine, and many houses dedicated to poor women and children were instituted by women's colleges and groups. In the Edwardian era, the poor had begun to take a role in their own reform, and many settlement halls were the site of debates and lectures run by working class men.

Also attracting interest for their dedication to social reform: the Fabian Society. Founded also in 1884, it became preeminent society for English socialism in the Edwardian era. Sidney and Beatrice Webb wrote many pamphlets and studies of the poor and of industrial Britain, and lobbied for the types of reforms popularized by Lloyd George—minimum wage, universal health care, and old age pensions. Famous Fabians included Virginia Woolf, H.G. Wells, Annie Besant, and George Bernard Shaw, the last of whom imbued many of his plays with his political beliefs. Lectures and public speaking engagements at Essex Hall were always packed, and gave a voice to the Labour Party.

This transformation from Victorian sentimentalism was extraordinary, and though many supported traditional class structure, an increasing number of people considered actions better than words when it came to social change. The people at the top may not have realized it, but society had begun to move beyond them long before WWI.

Domestic Servants
Edwardians of means and/or status could not function without servants. The basics of everyday life—heating, lighting, cooking, cleaning, and washing—were all incredibly labor intensive, and the presence of housemaids, parlourmaids, cooks, scullery maids, footmen, butlers, etc were also a status symbol, for they represented a particular level of income.

There was no shortage of prospective servants, with the 1901 census showing that a little over two million women out of the total British population of thirty-seven million were employed in domestic service, and the 1911 census showing an increase to 2.1 million servants out of a population of forty-one million. Compared with factory workers and farmers, whose wages were less than forty shillings (from which 2/3rds were spent on food), domestic servants, who were provided with board and lodging, did better on the whole (the usual allowance of food for each servant per week was 1/2 lb. of butter, 1/4 lb. of tea, 1 lb. of loaf sugar, 1 lb. of cheese, and a daily pint of beer. There was no restriction as to bread, but many ruled that all bread must be a day old before it was eaten).

The butler was the senior servant in the household who kept charge of the wine cellar, the serving of meals, the silver, and the general arrangements for the reception of guests. He saw to the fires in the sitting rooms, attended to his employer's literary needs so far as newspapers are concerned, and acted as valet to his master if no valet was kept. A butler's average wages ranged from £50 to £100.

The housekeeper was the senior female servant, who supervised the women staff (though she knew better than to meddle with either the cook or the nanny), was responsible for the cleaning and the laundry, and presented the menus daily to the mistress of the house for her approval. A housekeeper was invariably called "Mrs." because of the relative power/prestige possessed by a married woman. Her wages averaged £40-70 per year.

The cook ruled the kitchen and the kitchen- and scullery-maids beneath her. A cook's wages varied from £18 a year to £500 or more, and their duties in the household were quite as varied as their pay. The dining-room was her special charge, and to this was usually added the care of the hall, the doorsteps, and the kitchen staircase, in addition to her own special realm. She was also a "Mrs." whether married or not, or known informally as "Cook." Some homes employed a *chef de cuisine* (male) instead of a cook (female), and his wages could be astronomical when compared to hers. Rosa Lewis's reputation was an anomaly only because she was placed on equal footing with a chef.

With an average wage of £35-50 per year, the valet attended exclusively to the personal accommodation of his master. He waited upon him during all times of dressing and undressing; brushes, folds up his clothes, or places them in readiness for him. He saw to all repairs and put away clothes in a wardrobe when not in use, making sure to cover them with brown holland or linen wrappers to secure them from dust. Boots and shoes were cleaned by the under-footman, but each morning the valet placed them in the dressing-room for his master. While the housemaid cleaned the grate, lit the fire, and swept and dusted the room, he prepared the washing-table, arranged the shaving apparatus, and laid his master's clothing out for the day.

The sole responsibility of a lady's maid was to her mistress. Her duties were solely to care for the wardrobe of her mistress, to assist her at her toilette, to draw her bath, to lay out her clothes and keep her room tidy. Excellent sewing skills were a must, for the lady's maid repaired her mistress's clothing and hats, and was expected to smarten her attire when trips to the local seamstress or a fashionable dressmaker was either too expensive or too far away. A lady's maid also received her mistress's cast-offs, which, if sold to rag-pickers, could be a lucrative bonus to her annual wages of £20-30.

The head housemaid had charge of the linen and tidied the bedrooms of the lady and the gentleman of the house and a few of the spare rooms. A housemaid's wages ranged from £15 to £30, but an under-housemaid seldom exceeded £20—though sometimes where three or four were kept the second housemaid was paid highly, the wages of the first being in proportion. The under-housemaid was secondary to the head housemaid. Her duties were rather similar to the latter, though she lacked the opportunity to possess any real responsibility.

The duties of the first footman were as follows: he set the table for each meal, or brought the breakfast trays to the members of the family, other than his master and mistress, and attended to the front door during the morning. He rubbed up the silver daily, cleaning it thoroughly once a week, and kept the dining room in order. He attended to the lamps and lighting of the family fires, and after dinner, carried coffee to the library or drawing-room. When waiting on table, he passed the large dishes and gravies.

The second footman alternated with the first footman in attendance on the door. He cleaned the halls, took care of the breakfast and coatroom, served the children's table–should there be one–and attended to the dusting of high places. He occasionally helped to clean the silver and dishes, and when waiting on the table, he passed the vegetables, salad, and dessert, and after dinner, the cigarettes and cigars to the guests. The wages of footmen depended far more upon height and appearance than efficiency. A second footman of 5'6 would command £20-22, while one of 5'10 or 6 feet would not take under £28 or £30. A short first footman could not expect more than £30, while a tall man could command £32-40.

The lot of a scullery maid was tough. She rose the earliest in the house (sometimes as early as 4 am) to clean the grates and lay the household fires. But mostly, she was expected to wait on the cook, to wash up all pots, pans, dishes, plates, knives, forks, etc, to lay the table for the servants' meals, to wash vegetables, peel potatoes, and carry coals to the kitchen, and scullery. Her duties also consisted of sweeping the kitchen and scullery, dusting everything before the cook came down in the morning, and also charge of the front-door steps, area steps and area. For all of this, her wages ranged from £10-14 per year.

The position of chauffeur was relatively new in 1912, which meant his duties–and pay–varied based on the house and employer. He also existed in the in-between world occupied by the governess, since he was not a member of the household, yet he was not a member of the outdoor servants (and those employed in the stables tended to resent the presence of an automobile and the changes it entailed). At best, the chauffeur's duties consisted of driving the family and of maintaining the upkeep of the motorcar, and with board and lodgings included, his wages ranged from a lowly £10 to a very high £250, if he were very experienced.

In her memoirs, *Before The Sunset Fades* (1953), Daphne Fielding, ex-Marchioness of Bath, detailed the forty-three member staff employed at Longleat during the Edwardian era:

> One House Steward
> One Butler
> One Under Butler
> One Groom of the Chambers
> One Valet
> Three Footmen
> One Steward's Room Footman
> Two Oddmen
> Two Pantry Boys
> One Lamp Boy
> One Housekeeper
> Two Lady's Maids
> One Nurse
> One Nursery Maid
> Eight Housemaids
> Two Sewing Maids
> Two Still Room Maids
> Six Laundry Maids
> One Chef
> Two Kitchen Maids
> One Vegetable Maid
> One Scullery Maid
> One Daily Woman

Such a large staff was not typical amongst all great country houses, but the scope and scale of the house, not to mention the entertainments and house parties and fetes held on the estate, required a large staff of mostly invisible employees to keep everything humming along. Outside staff usually comprised of coachmen, grooms, stable boys, gardeners, gamekeepers, and later the chauffeur/mechanic. Some households even hired their own dairymaids, who churned the butter, milked the cows (though some localities employed cowkeepers for this task), watched the cheeses, and made the cream. Included in the wages of domestic servants were allowances for beer, sugar, and tea, and they given annual gifts of cloth with which to make up their uniforms.

A further anecdote in Daphne Fielding's reminisces included the average day for servants in a country estate like Longleat:

- Each week three sheep of different species were butchered for the household, one Southdown, one Westmorland, and one Brittany, the last being used exclusively for small cutlets.
- Every morning the chef wrote out the menus on a broad slate and took them upstairs for the approval of Lady Bath.
- When the family moved to Berkeley Square for the London Season, seventeen of the staff accompanied them, together with eleven horses and five stablemen.
- The housekeeper and the house steward presided over the steward's room table at which the head butler, the cook, the lady's maids, the valets and the groom of the chambers used to eat. The remainder, the liveried servants and the under maids, had their meals in the servants' hall where the second butler and head laundry maid ranked the highest. The housekeeper had her own sitting room where she received the steward's room for tea.
- Twice a week, on Tuesdays and Thursdays, dances were held in the servants' hall. A pianist was engaged from the neighboring town and a buffet supper was produced by the kitchen and still room staff.
- The normal day at Longleat began with prayers before breakfast, at which the whole family appeared. The staff entered the chapel in single file in order of precedence. The village clergyman officiated.

- The first footman was considered to be the Lady's footman. It was he who stood behind her chair, and any chore that the Lady's maid required to have done for her mistress was his responsibility. The third footman was the nursery footman, at the beck and call of the nannies.
- The duty of the groom of the chambers was to care for the reception rooms, see that the writing tables were properly equipped, collect letters for the post, deliver notes and messages, look after the fires and attend to the comfort and needs of the visitors.

And all of this is just a fraction of the lives and duties of the domestic servants. Some stately homes, like the magnificent Chatsworth or Blenheim Palace, possessed even more staff, all of whom kept the great estates running smoothly and unobtrusively.

Much further down on the social scale, etiquette books and authors who advised on household management, such as Mrs. Beeton, gave this advice on the recommended number or variety of domestic servants one could afford based on income:
About £1,000 a year—A cook, upper housemaid, nursemaid, under housemaid, and a man servant.
About £750 a year—A cook, housemaid, nursemaid, and footboy.
About £500 a year—A cook, housemaid, and nursemaid.
About £300 a year—A maid-of-all-work and nursemaid.
About £200 or £150 a year—A maid-of-all-work (and girl occasionally).

By the mid-Edwardian era, legislation was introduced to protect the rights of domestic servants, and the 1911 National Insurance Act solidified their right to health care and respect from their employers. Though the First World War did not break the tradition or need for servants, pre-war housewives had long been admonished by women's journals and newspapers and books about self-sufficiency, and the invention of household appliances gradually chipped away at the dependence on servants. Nevertheless, the character of the country house, or even the London mansion, was largely created by its large staff, and being "In Service" was considered a coveted position for the lower classes for a surprisingly long period in history.

Fashion & Shopping
Until the 1920s, when the combination of artificial fabrics and working-class girls with wartime salaries to burn resulted in a booming ready-to-wear (or off-the-peg) market, clothes were a clear marker of the haves and the have-nots.

In the 1850s and 1860s, ladies wore those large crinolines, lavish silks and satins, and tons of ribbons and flowers to display their husband's wealth, and this continued to be true into the Edwardian era. The silhouette was also influenced by social changes: the elaborate bustles of the 1880s supposed to signify a woman's fertility in that lean decade; the extreme leg-o-mutton sleeves of 1893-1896 representing the athleticism of the New Woman; the S-curve corset of the early 1900s a return to extreme femininity; and the hobble skirt of the 1910s to literally hobble women just as they began their radical fight for independence and the vote.

"....A large fraction of our time was spent in changing our clothes." said Cynthia Asquith, and during the Edwardian era, men and women were expected to change multiple times a day, depending on their activity, the season, and their residence. A typical wardrobe for an upper class lady consisted of ball gowns, tea gowns, tailor-mades (neat, tailored suits), evening gowns, morning gowns, and walking suits--and this is before she was required to purchase specific attire for specific sporting activities (bicycling, fox hunting, etc).

Men were no different, requiring morning dress--no gentleman would be seen in anything but a tailcoat, waistcoat, top hat, gloves, and gray striped trousers before 1 PM--evening dress, various styles of coats, tweed suits and Norfolk jackets, linen suits for summer, and his own attire for various sporting activities.

The West End was the shopping mecca in which these items were acquired. According to a 1902 guide to London, "a very convenient starting point for shopping is Charing Cross...you are in the time-honoured central circle of West End London, whence the four-mile cab system radiates." These shops, situated around Bond Street, Regent Street, Piccadilly, Oxford Street, Knightsbridge, Buckingham Palace Road, Kensington High Street, and Westbourne Grove, provided everything for the well-to-do, from gloves and hats and walking sticks, to carpets and cutlery, to jewelry and hosiery.
In the Re
gency era, Bond Street was the sole province of men's goods, but it expanded in the Victorian era, with Old Bond Street being the home of longtime men's tailors, hatmakers, and bootmakers, and New Bond Street more geared towards women shoppers, with their own shops as well as tea rooms. Bond Street held tightly to its aristocratic pedigree and was the only street onto which nothing but foot and carriage traffic were allowed.

A shopping trip to London was considered an all-day pursuit, and tea rooms and ladies clubs sprang up to accommodate lady shoppers--the former allowing ladies to break the taboo of dining in public and without a male escort, and the latter giving ladies a place to relax, play cards, write letters, and even smoke, just like in a gentleman's club. The best time to shop, according to a 1912 handbook, was in June, when one could receive the best bargains just as the Season came to a close.

The department store, with its ready-made frocks, was largely the province of the upper middle classes, but English ladies were just as tempted by its bargains and advertisements--and wealthy Americans, accustomed to stopping Macy's or Wanamaker's, made them somewhat fashionable. As a result, Harrods and Selfridges went all out in lavishness and luxury to attract the tentative aristocratic clientele, and remain top of the line today.

Though the wealthy visited Paris to replenish their wardrobes, the average aristocratic lady relied upon old-fashioned court dressmakers and the needles of their lady's maids to keep their wardrobes up to date. Soon, however, Parisian couture houses opened up London branches to take advantage of Americans in residence, and they no doubt encouraged their titled friends to step inside the ateliers of Lanvin, Worth, and Poiret.

Chapter 8: Edwardians Eat

Edwardian Gastronomy
According to British restaurant critic, Giles Coren, "a hundred years ago, British food was in its golden age, with the arrival of the great restaurant, the celebrity chef, exotic new dishes, and gargantuan twelve course meals." Leading the way was, of course, King Edward VII. When Prince of Wales, he had swept aside both the lengthy meal times, encouraged service à la russe, and introduced, via his great appetite, the trend for copious, rich, luxurious eating habits. By the time he came to the throne, "his aristocratic and upper middle-class subjects were set on an annual collision course with raging dyspepsia."

The restaurant dinner, popular in Paris since the time of the French Revolution, had reached British shores by the 1880s. At first the act of dining in public was viewed warily–gentlemen were already accustomed to dining away from home at their clubs, men of the middle-class in steak shops and those of the working-class at oyster shops or food stands along the streets. For ladies, the thought of eating in a place where strangers could gawk and stare was abhorrent. The breaking down of social barriers contributed to the custom of "dining out" by the 1890s. No longer were private, in-home suppers indicative of who was "in" and who was "out", and both ladies and gentlemen eagerly partook of the opportunity to leave their homes to see and be seen in the glamorous setting of a restaurant of the highest class.

To cater to this influx of diners, luxury hotels such as Claridge's, the Cecil, the Ritz and the Savoy, began to remodel their dining rooms into chic restaurants, fitted with terraced dining, winter gardens and separate supper rooms for private parties. An American influence came with the introduction of the "bar" and the "grillroom", which was a room set aside for informal dining. The advent of this new transatlantic society left one restaurant clinging to the English tradition of formal evening attire. To dine in the Savoy's restaurant, or even to be served coffee in the adjoining foyer, it was absolutely essential that a lady wore a dinner gown sans chapeau and her escort a dress suit. Anyone who did not follow this command was liable to be refused entry, as an earl and his countess were to discover one night in 1907.

With these restaurants came the celebrity chef. Not since Antoine Carême ruled the stomachs of the Regency era's celebrities had the British shores experienced the artistry of a chef de haute cuisine. His successor? Auguste Escoffier, a Nice-born chef who simplified and modernized Carême's methods and contributed to the development of modern French cuisine. Escoffier formed a partnership with Cesar Ritz in 1890, and the two men moved to the Savoy Hotel in London and from there, established numerous hotels, including the Hotel Ritz across the world. In 1898, they opened the Hotel Ritz in Paris, and The Carlton in London the following year, where Escoffier also introduced the practice of the à la carte menu.

Escoffier had a rival in the form of a woman: the former scullery maid and proud Cockney, Rosa Lewis. The proprietress of the Cavendish Hotel, she had begun her culinary career in the London house of the Comte de Paris, the Orleanist pretender to the French throne. From there she went from the kitchens of the Duc d'Aumale, to the Duc d'Orleans, and at one time, simultaneously controlled the kitchens of White's Club and W.W. Astor's home, Hever Castle. It was when Lady Randolph Churchill acquired Rosa's services that she began her ascent to fame. Anecdotes tell of the Prince of Wales, upon being introduced to Rosa by Lady Randolph as an excellent cook, never doubted it, exclaiming "Damme, she takes more pains with a cabbage than with a chicken. . . . She gives me nothing sloppy, nothing colored up to dribble on a man's shirt-front."

Rosa became the first freelance cook, and was available for hire by any person who could afford her services. With Bertie's endorsement and her food witness to her talent, she became much in demand, with hostesses vying to obtain her services for country house parties throughout England. As she grew in importance, Rosa began to travel about with a chorus of assistant cooks attired exactly as she was, in spotless white with tall chef's hats and high laced "cooking boots" of soft black kid, to support the ankles during the long hours spent preparing dishes.

During the Coronation year of 1902, Rosa produced 29 suppers for just as many large balls, and often came home in the wee hours of the morning without a wink of sleep. With the money saved from that year, she bought the Cavendish Hotel in Jermyn Street, where she earned a fortune catering to the vital needs of the aristocracy: privacy and excellent food. A private dining room was available for use, where swells could bring their lady friends, and there were permanent suites for those inclined to live outside of their homes.

Exotic dishes were created to meet the demand from aristocratic gourmands. The ultimate Edwardian recipe? A rich, extravagant dish comprised of pate de fois gras stuffed inside of a truffle, which was stuffed inside of an ortolan, itself stuffed inside of a quail. Escoffier invented the Pêche Melba and Melba Toast in the 1890s, both dishes named for the strident soprano Nellie Melba, and Rosa Lewis invented a delicious quail pudding for King Edward.

Because meal times were pushed back by the close of the 19th century, other, smaller meals were inserted into the day to fill rumbling bellies. Lunch was inserted between breakfast and dinner, ladies added the afternoon tea. Another sort of tea–with hot muffins, crumpets, toast, cold salmon, pies, ham, roast beef, fruit, cream and tea and coffee–found its way into the more active and informal program of the country house.

The Edwardians never stopped eating. From the time they rose, to even the times they awoke in the middle of the night, food was ready and available. A typical English breakfast consisted of haddock, kidneys, kedgeree, porridge, game pie, tongue, poached eggs, bacon, chicken and woodcock. Luncheon included hot and cold dishes: cold fowls, lamb, pigeon, cold pie and ptarmigan, puddings, cheeses, biscuits, jellies, and fruit.

Supper now served *à la russe*, this allowed a greater sample of dishes available, and the number of courses grew. During the height of the Edwardian period, to sit down for a ten to fifteen course meal was quite the norm. Of course one wasn't required to partake of each course, nor was it expected, but the parade of dishes: hors d'oeuvres, soups, salads, vegetables, meats– poultry, game, beef, mutton, and pork–, seafood, puddings, breads, savories, and fruits, if not the number of wines offered to compliment each course, is enough to make our 21st century stomachs queasy.

And it didn't end there. Hostesses expecting the King were well advised to provide snacks consisting of lobster salad and cold chicken to serve at eleven, and even after dinner, a plate of sandwiches, and sometimes a quail or cutlet, was sent to his rooms. At night, dainties were left outside of guests' rooms during country house parties, in case someone felt a bit peckish. Despite the expense put into creating these elaborate meals, those of smaller means weren't left out of the general smörgåsbord.

This was also the apogee of name brands and modern processed foods such as Marmite (1902), Ty.phoo tea (1904), Colman's Mustard (1903), bouillon cubes made simulate beef extract by Maggi (1908) and Oxo (1910), instant coffee (1901), Bird's Custard Powder (est. 1837), Jacob's water biscuits (1881), HP Sauce (1903) and Cadbury's Milk Chocolate (est. 1824). The appearance of refrigeration made dining much easier too.

This trend for gargantuan meals obviously had its downsides. At the end of the season, these Edwardian gastronomes found their digestion so wound in knots, a month-long jaunt to the Continent was deemed necessary. And the annual trek to

Austrian or German watering spots like Bad-Ischl or Carlsbad, were added to the general round of the season. Here ladies and gentlemen were put on strict diets and forced to exercise daily. At the end of the treatment, or "cure", they would return to their homes a bit trimmer and with better digestion, only to begin the round of eating once more. Fortunately for the ladies, the standards of beauty praised the ample, womanly curves created by nature and enhanced with corsets, which gave them the signature "S" shape most assiduously admired by the men of the period.

English Food and Drink
English cooking had a bad rap during the 19th and early 20th centuries. Caricatures of the typical Englishman ("John Bull") poked fun at his florid face, his avoirdupois, and his bad manners when eating a meal consisting of a joint and boiled vegetables. In contrast, the typical Frenchman was even-complected, with a graceful figure, and impeccable and elegant table manners as he sat to dine at six course meal of the most aromatic and delicately prepared dishes.

The mania for French cooking began with Antonin Carême, chef de cuisine to the Prince Regent, who simplified meals and organized dishes into distinct groups, and solidified under Alexis Soyer, whose feasts dominated the imaginations of the early Victorians. French haute cuisine reached its pinnacle beneath the magical fingers of Auguste Escoffier, who became one of the leaders in the development of modern French cuisine. Yet, beneath the canapés and ragoûts, traditional English cooking retained its position on the tables of not only the poor and working classes, but on the menus of aristocratic and royal houses.

Traditional English cuisine was influenced by England's Puritan roots, which shunned strong flavors and the complex sauces associated with European (Catholic) nations. Most dishes, such as bread and cheese, roasted and stewed meats, meat and game pies, boiled vegetables and broths, and freshwater and saltwater fish, had ancient origins, and recipes for the aforementioned existed in the Forme of Cury, a 14th century cook book dating from the royal court of Richard II. Not surprisingly, English cuisine had its regional dishes, the most famous being Cornwall's Stargazy Pie, Derbyshire's Bakewell tart, Lancashire's hot pot, Leicestershire's Stilton cheese, and Devonshire's clotted cream.

An Englishman was most proud of his meat and game, and even after dining à la russe surpassed service à la française in popularity, the host of a supper party considered carving a roast or a joint or a fish an art, and practically a divine right to show off at the table. In historical fiction, the meat most often mentioned is mutton.

Though meat in its various incarnations are typically described in an unappetizing manner, in truth, mutton is to lamb what beef to is veal—that is, meat from a sheep older than two years—and far from being cold and congealed and otherwise disgusting, mutton was very versatile: one could boil it, broil it, bake it, roast it, fillet it, stew it, braise it, and fry it.

Due to game laws, other extremely popular meats such as venison, hare, partridge, pigeon, and pheasant, and so on, were restricted to the wealthy, since the land on which game (and the lakes and rivers where fish was found) were owned by English aristocrats or the Royal Family, and shooting and hunting permits were expensive. However, the Sunday roast, a traditional meal served on that day and consisting of "roasted meat, roast potato together with accompaniments, such as Yorkshire pudding, stuffing, vegetables and gravy," was a meal common in all English households, with variations depending upon taste and budget.

Another most English dish is pudding. This was not the familiar milk-based chocolate or tapioca Jell-O brand seen in American supermarkets, but a rich, starchy, and typically savoury dish. Some puddings, such as rice pudding or Christmas pudding, were for dessert, but the best-known (Yorkshire pudding, suet pudding, blood pudding, etc) derived from English cooks devising ways in which to utilize fat drippings or leftover meats or blood.

During the British Raj, English cooks began to borrow from Indian dishes, creating a fusion cuisine known as "Anglo-Indian." By the end of the 19th century, Kedgeree, Mulligatawny soup, curried meats, and chutney became such a staple on the English menu, the dishes were absorbed into the national English cuisine.

But let us not forget that most English of cuisine: Tea! Though tea was drunk in vast quantities by the English since the 17th century, it was when afternoon tea was devised by the Duchess of Bedford in the 1840s, that tea consumption increased. In 1911 alone, the people of the United Kingdom as a whole, consumed 296,000,000 pounds, or six and three-quarters pounds per person, of tea!!! Only Russia, which consumed 147,132,000 pounds of tea came close to that figure. Strangely enough, the French considered tea a medicinal drink, preferring coffee, though ardent Anglophiles gamely indulged in their "fif o'clock."

Consumed with the tea were scones (Scottish in origin); dropped scones (which look like small pancakes) dipped in honey, crumpets (which look like English muffins); pikelets ("a British regional dialect word variously denoting a flatter variant on crumpet or muffin. In the West Midlands [and to some extent, the Yorkshire area] it is a term for crumpet. A crumpet in this area is similar in appearance [but not taste] to a North American pancake; light sandwiches (watercress, cucumber, ham, etc); and small cakes and pastries, all of which were displayed on tiered stands.

Another form of tea was the "high tea," which does not denote a fancy tea party, but a somewhat substantial meal of cold meats, tea, cakes, and sandwiches. Farming or working-class families mostly ate this, though, as the supper hour was pushed back to the late evening in the Edwardian era, English people of all classes tended to indulge.

And so, English cooking, despite its preponderance of heavy meats, savory delights, and brow-raising names (Toad-in-a-hole, anyone?), is far from deserving of its bad reputation. After all, many of our most famous English (and American) heroes and heroines dined daily upon these dishes and I feel secure knowing that Jane Austen, Anne Bronte, and Charles Dickens wrote their masterpieces nourished by their Mother Country's cooking.

Luncheon, according to Lady Colin Campbell, has been defined as an insult to one's breakfast and an outrage to one's dinner. For most of the 19th century, three meals—breakfast, dinner, and supper—were considered sufficient, but the shift in dinner time to later in the day called something more substantial than a glass of madeira and a slice of madeira cake. This small meal was first called "nooning", and was consumed during the regular visiting hours of Regency era ladies (between 11 and 4).

By the 1850s, "lunch" or "luncheon" became a part of the standard meal times of the day, and by the 1880s, society witnessed a plethora of lunches: hunting lunches, race luncheons, shooting luncheons, etc.
Etiquette, of course, sprang around this new mealtime. According to Mrs. Humphry:
> "The toilettes of the ladies are also more like dinner dresses than those usually worn in the afternoon. Here, with us, ordinary afternoon dress is the rule for ladies. In town, in the season, a man is expected to Luncheons wear either a frockcoat or a cutaway black coat. If he has been regularly invited to lunch he leaves his hat and stick in the hall. In the country, a man wears a country suit, or riding dress if he has ridden from his own home to his hostess' house.
> All the guests are shown into the drawing room, where the hostess receives them. They retain their hats and, in winter, leave furs or heavy wraps in the hall or dining room. Gloves are usually removed and Guest when sitting down to table. The hostess may or may not have

hat or bonnet on. If she has just come in from shopping or driving, she very probably will be in outdoor dress. At a very formal luncheon, however, she will be in indoor dress; since outdoor costume might be interpreted as having reference to some intention of going out immediately after, and would be considered as a hint to her guests to leave early.

The routine of the meal is very simple. When the table is laid, all cold dishes are placed upon it, so as to have the service simplified as much as possible. One of the charms of lunch is that the servants are not in the room after the sweets have been brought in and handed round. In some houses, when the meal is a very elaborate one, the servants remain to hand fruit or ices, but the general custom is for them to leave the room and shut the door, having left everything ready in the shape of plates, knives, forks, spoons, &c. The meal is never expected to be a very elaborate one. Soup or fish may precede a joint or an entree, or a dish of game. The joint is getting quite unfashionable among the smart. Rather small chicken pies or dishes of a French character are more acceptable than anything heavy or solid. Where the minage is of an important kind, the carving is done by the butler at a side-table, just as it is at dinner. Wine is not so much drunk at lunch as it used to be. Claret is, however, generally at hand. At many tables aerated waters are the usual beverage at this meal, even in houses where wine is always served at dinner. When gentlemen are present, they often like a glass of beer at luncheon. But even when no wine is habitually used, wineglasses are laid at each cover, which is prepared exactly as for dinner.

There is now such a rage for champagne that many people would regard a lunch as very incomplete without that wine. The hostess has to consider all these various views and decide what course she shall take in the matter.

The meal over...the rest of the party adjourn to the dining-room where coffee is usually served, and it is generally half-past three or nearly four before the guests leave. When guests are leaving, the hostess rings the bell, and sometimes walks with them as far as the drawing-room door. The servants have presumably been trained to hand each lady her coat and sunshade or umbrella; each gentleman his hat, overcoat, stick or umbrella; also to call a cab or summon the carriage, as the case may be.

The working classes kept to the three meal tradition of breakfast, supper, and dinner, mostly because they hadn't the leisure time to spare and since they worked early and went to bed early. Supper was also called High Tea, or Meat Tea in northern England and Scotland (though in common vernacular, it was just Tea), which typically consisted of "tea with sugar, bread heaped with butter, jam, preserves, cold meat, cheese or an egg."

Among the poorer classes, the meal might be nothing more than a pot of tea with a bloater or herring, but on excursions or on holidays, "it might become the occasion for eating fish and chips, a dish which, it has been claimed, originated in Oldham in the 1860s."

As stated before, the English had drunk tea since the 17th century, but the Duchess of Bedford popularized afternoon tea in the 1840s. This ritual spread down and up the social ladder (with the exception of the poor and working classes) until it became an expression of one's leisure time and social status. Afternoon tea served multiple purposes, all of which had little to do with a repast before dinner.

Lady Colin Campbell's etiquette book lists two classes of tea—great tea and little tea, the latter which comprised of "handed tea" or "afternoon tea", and "high" or "meat" teas in the former (this was shared by the rich and poor, but was considered more a country entertainment than an actual necessary meal by the rich).

The High or Meat tea described by Lady Colin was considerably more substantial than the one eaten by the poor: "bowls of old china filled with ripe red strawberries, and jugs of rich cream by their side. Glass dishes containing preserved fruits of different colours, such as apricots, strawberries, marmalade, &c., take their stands at short intervals. Cakes of various kinds—plum, rice, and sponge; and then within easy reach of the "tea-drinkers" are hot muffins, crumpets, toast, tea-cakes, and what not.

At one end of the table the tea-tray stands, with its adjuncts; at the other the coffee is placed, also on a tray. The sideboard is the receptacle of the weightier matters, such as cold salmon, pigeon and veal and ham pies, boiled and roast fowls, tongues, ham, veal cake; and should it be a very 'hungry tea,' roast beef and lamb may be there for the gentlemen of the party."
There were also servants in attendance, who carved the meat and prepared the tea, and frequently this meal was capped by a small dance or a game of charades.

The Handed, or Afternoon tea, was part of a lady's "At Home", which was the designated hour and day when she would receive callers. If so inclined, one would drop by for tea and find the hostess in the drawing room where she served tea to her callers and provided food of a daintier fare: "In winter, muffins and hot buttered cakes, sometimes buttered toast, are provided, with mixed biscuits and tempting looking little cakes from the confectioner's. Plain bread and butter, brown and white, are always provided, and the slices are usually rolled so that they can be lifted without the glove or finger coming in contact with the butter. Foie gras sandwiches are always appreciated, and in summer sandwiches made of cucumber or cress are liked."

Alcoholic beverages were just as commonplace as tea, with beer and ale the staple of the working glasses, and fine wines the province of the wealthy. During the Edwardian period, cocktails—the American influence—invaded English restaurants and homes, and according to a 1910 issue of The

Sketch, the smartest homes served them before lunch or dinner. Punches, mixed drinks containing fruit or fruit juice, with the option of alcohol, were de rigueur for balls where large amounts of drink were needed to quench hundreds of thirsty dancers.

Other drinks popular with the Edwardians were coffee (though not as popular as it was in America and in France), champagne, and aerated (mineral) water. The last of these rose in stature with the growth of health consciousness and the fad for hiking and mountaineering. The most popular brand was Perrier, a company owned by Sir Saint-John Harmsworth, the younger brother of Lord Northcliffe of the *Daily Mail*. He launched a huge campaign in his brother's papers touting the chicness and Frenchness of the aerated water to the *Daily Mail*'s readership. Soon bottled mineral water flooded the market, and the 1907 Army & Navy Catalog lists two pages worth of brands.

The Etiquette of Dining

The evolution of formal dining begins in the medieval era, where dining became a sign of social status. At that time, the table setting included the Salt Cellar, which was the first thing put on the table. The salt was far more than a condiment–to sit above the salt was to sit in the place of honor, and until the salt was put upon the table, no one could know where would be his allotted seat.

Then came the silver dishes for holding vegetable or fish, sometimes meat, and small loaves of bread. However, spoons and knives were not furnished by the host, but were brought by guests whose servants, so equipped, cut the meat and carved the food for each person. The guests had no plates or forks and few knives, but ate with their hands and threw the refuse on the floors, but the cleanliness of the cloth, or Nappe, was of paramount importance and a matter of great pride.

As the nobility began to express its wealth in its silver trenchers, wassail bowls, ewers, lavers, basins and other implements and tools of the table, eating became less egalitarian and the classes stratified based on their table settings. Spoons were also brought by guests, and these elaborately designed silver utensils were often gifts of one of the sponsors at baptism, a practice which most likely spawned the phrase "born with a silver spoon."

Forks came later, and their introduction produced much criticism, the objectors holding that "fingers were made before forks." They came from Italy, and the early 17th century correspondence of Thomas Coryat cite the new discovery as almost as important as the discover of America, and causing far more discussion.

By the reign of Charles II, forks were in common use. The fork did much for the simplification and advancement of culinary art by encouraging the taste for solid viands and natural flavors.

The use of the fork made possible the delicate slice as against the gobbets of meat of the century before, and also, the fork promoted cleanliness at the table. It also made possible choicer table linen, finer clothes and handsome napkins, and there soon developed definite rules for folding and laying the napkin so that there was published diagrams showing twenty-five ways to fold a napkin.

Knives, forks, spoons, platters, ewers and basins created a custom for a more dignified setting of table, and with these new table appliances, manners improved and culinary art advanced to higher standards, the better to fit the richer and more elaborate table setting and silver service. By the 18th century, more attractive and stately service were developed, and silversmiths were set at work to achieve higher standards of art in metalwork.

Finer woodwork and other metal works developed concurrently, and as the wealthy, the noble, and the royal began to fill their houses with costly, exquisite goods, their table settings became more elaborate as well until dining became a pageant in its own right. Vast, elaborate meals became a way to assert power, wealth and status, and they moved back into public view. But this time, with the arrival of the Dutch practice of alternating seating for the sexes, women sat at the table on equal footing with men.

Service *à la française*, whereby separate courses were created rather than two or three courses, where everything alike was lumped together, took hold of the gustatory habits of the wealthy at the turn of the 19th century. This imposed new rules on the order in which food was to be served; the theories of Carême and Brillat-Savarin felt that the foods' relationships to one another were an important element of the dining experience, and both believed food should be served in this order: soup, fish, meat, game, sweets and fruits, and the side dishes were to complement these main items.

This method was better than the previous methods of serving diners, but it was difficult to keep the dishes hot by the time they reached the table from the far-away kitchen. Because of this, service à la française was rendered impractical, making room for service *à la russe*, or service in the Russian style, which was brought to France in 1811 by the Russian ambassador.

However, this style of service did not catch on in England or America until the 1860s and 1870s, where the English style of service (all the food belonging to one course is placed in suitable dishes before the host or hostess and served from the table) was more prevalent. With the Russian style of service, there was greater emphasis on the presentation of both meals and place settings.

Now, when guests arrived to be seated for dinner, there were place cards designating where one would sit, a menu provided from which one would choose the dishes to eat during each course, and rather than sitting to a table laden down with chafing dishes and platters of food, there was a simple "cover," which consisted of the plates, glasses, silver and napkin to be used by each person.

With this new emphasis on table setting, as with the influx of the newly rich knocking at the doors of the upper classes giving rise to etiquette books, service à la russe created a set of rigid, correct rules for cutlery, china and table adornments.

The table now cleared of food, table setting blended four elements of design: central decorations, flowers, color, and mirrors. Central decoration usually consisted of epergnes or plateaus, the latter of which was a raised mirror, often with silver or gilt decorations on the raised sides, while the former was a tall stand with hanging arms that held either baskets of sweets, or platforms that held glasses containing sweets.

The custom of placing flowers on the dining table began in the early 19th century, but by the turn of the century, the use of a heavy candelabra and elevated dishes alternating with low dishes took hold. Large masses of flowers often covered the table, nearly crowding out the place settings, and often the individual places were delineated by strands of ivy or other flowers strung between each cover.

Color was important to the early- and mid-Victorians, and colored table runners, color glasses such as green hock glasses or ruby-colored wine glasses, added a deep splash of color against the already crowded table.

Added to this were mirrors, which generally reflected peaceful scenes if a mirrored plateau with figures was not being used. The Edwardian era saw a streamlining of the table setting, and the table was cleared of the masses of flowers and other accouterments in favor of a simple arrangement of candelabra, bowls of fruit and flower arrangements set one after the other along the length of the table. Now, instead of candles, small lamps, shaded by delicate lampshades, cast an intimate glow across the dining table and its diners.

Beneath the table decorations lay the more important articles of gastronomy: the tablecloth, the dishes, and the silverware. Maids setting the table for dinner were instructed to first lay the silence cloth (of double-faced cotton flannel, knitted table padding, or an asbestos pad) upon the table, then to lay the covers, allowing 24-30 inches from plate to plate.

If the table was bare, the covers were marked by plate doilies. A service plate was then laid for each person, one inch from the edge of the table, and this plate remained upon the table until it was necessary to replace it with a hot plate. The silver placed in the order which it was to be used, beginning at the outside and using toward the plate.

Silver for the dessert course was never put on with the silver required for other courses, except for the dinner which was served without a maid. Neither was the table set with more than three forks. If more were required, they were placed with their respective courses. The salad or dessert silver was brought either in on the plate, or placed beside a napkin or tray at the right, from the right, after the plate is placed. The knife or knives were placed at the right of the plate, half an inch from the edge of the table, with the cutting edge toward the plate.

Spoons, with bowls facing up, were placed at the right of the knife, and forks, with the tines turned upward, at the left of the plate. The spoon for fruit or the small fork for oysters or hors d'œuvre was placed at the extreme right or on the plate containing the course and the napkin was at the left of the forks, and the hem and selvage was required to parallel with the forks and the edge of the table. The water glass was placed at the point of the knife, the bread-and-butter plate above the service plate, and the butter spreader across the upper, right-hand side of the bread-and-butter plate. Salt and pepper sets were placed between each two covers.

During the heyday of service à la française, the sideboard was used to hold all extras required during the service of the meal.

The serving table took its place when the French service was replaced by the Russian, and the sideboard was used for decorative purposes only, usually holding choice pieces of silver.

Besides this new emphasis on table setting, the most important and enduring development derived from service a la russe was the matching of dishes to wines. Before, diners would eat and drink wines to their own tastes, but the Russian service, with its sparser table made it logical to serve a particular wine with each course. Due to this new protocol of complimentary food and wine, the types of and numbers of wine glasses the diner had to negotiate grew.

Now the opening oyster course was to be eaten accompanied by Chablis, the soup and also the hot hors d'œuvre with sherry, fish with hock, removes and entrees with champagne, the meat with burgundy, game with claret, and dessert with port, Tokay, or other fine wines. Cocktails later joined this group by the turn of the century, though the practice of having a cocktail before dinner did not emerge until the 1910s.

Needless to say, though the formal table setting has simplified much since the 19th century, the array of flatware, dishes and glasses remain formidable and continue to impose a barrier between the wealthy and the middle- and lower-classes. From this evolution of formal dining, we can see that though most do not dine with such elaborate courses or settings, the interest in food and eating has not abated in a thousand years.

Chapter 9: Social Transformations

Education
The Education Act of 1870 ensured that "every child would have a school place available to it in a building of reasonable quality and with a certified head teacher." For the first time ever, children of the working and lower-middle classes had access to education that was easily available, taught on a regular basis and at a certain standard, and best of all, free.

T.H.S. Escott's *Social Transformations of the Victorian* Age reiterates this monumental transformation in society: "[T]he 1870 Act at once partially enabled the child of the poorest parents to mount through the elementary schools, to the secondary schools of the Kingdom and thence to those seats of learning at which the picked youth of the country enjoy the choicest opportunities of mental culture, or are qualified for the highest posts in after life to which English ambition can aspire."

In these schools—never called "public school," a term reserved for the endowed boarding schools like Eton or Rugby—the typical subjects taught were English grammar, geography, history, mathematics, science, Latin, modern languages, and domestic economy. Granted, girls were unlikely to be taught the subjects deemed by society as "masculine," and were steered towards "feminine" subjects such as needlework and cooking; however, the curriculum was rigorous and thorough.

The early days of the Act were not smooth and carefree. It came up against two foes: religious institutions, who had traditionally been at the forefront of children's education, and were upset at their loss of power, and poor parents, who relied upon the income their children could produce, and were loath to force their children to keep up regular attendance. To mitigate the reaction of the former, board schools were deliberately non-sectarian, and for the latter, a new act passed in 1876 to make attendance compulsory for every child at least age 10, and thereafter aged 13 unless he or she could pass a special leaving examination.

The Act of 1880 finally made school compulsory for all children, with the minimum leaving age gradually raised, to eleven in 1893, and twelve in 1899, and in 1893, all Board schools were free. The 1890s and 1900s saw the transformation of public education from a privilege grudgingly given to those who could pay for it into a right for every child.

London in particular was at the forefront of this change, as the curriculum and scope widened to include music lessons, trips to museums, etiquette lessons, dancing, theatrical amusements, and games. The reforms were predictably met with skepticism and suspicion, since the education of the lower class was not really supposed to foster their imaginations or reasoning skills, but the school system marched on, intent upon building up the nation through the mind and body.

The progress of girls' education in the late Victorian and Edwardian eras was remarkable. For much of history, women, whether noble or of yeoman stock, were barred from more "strenuous" education than sewing, cleaning, and cooking. Even allowing the average woman to read and write more than the Bible and her name, respectively, was viewed with horror, and basic mathematics were likely to only be taught to a merchant's daughter or wife.

A highly educated woman was an anomaly, and even ladies were strongly against the education of their daughters: Lady Mary Wortley Montagu complained bitterly that "there is hardly a creature in the world more despicable and more liable to universal ridicule than that of a learned woman," while "folly is reckoned so much our proper sphere, we are sooner pardoned any excesses of that than the least pretensions to reading and good sense."

Eighteenth century feminist Hannah More deplored craze for turning out "accomplished daughters" amongst the lower-middle classes (aping the aristocracy), asserting that "a young lady may excel in speaking French and Italian, may repeat a few passages from a volume of extracts, play like a professor, and sing like a siren" and yet be very badly educated, if her mind remains untrained. Nevertheless, she, and other female supporters of women's education, remained marginalized, and attempts throughout the first half of the 19th century to give girls as rigorous an education as boys were intermittent and done on a small scale.

This changed in 1848 with the inauguration of Queen's College in London, which had formerly been the Governess's Benevolent Institution (est. 1843), under the aegis of Queen Victoria's Maids-of-Honour. Girls of the upper classes had long been educated by Swiss and German governesses due to the poor education of English young women, and it was determined to equip young women thrown by circumstance into the (limited) workforce with the education necessary to teach children. The most famous of these early women's colleges was Cheltenham Ladies' College (est. 1853), which, under Dorothea Beale, became the prototype for advanced education.

By the 1860s, the best ladies colleges were brought in close connection with Oxford and Cambridge, and the introduction of entrance examinations and the opening of other universities to women students led to the formation of women's universities in their own right.

Lady Margaret Hall was founded in 1878, Somerville College in 1879, Miss Beale founded St. Hilda's in 1885, and St Hugh's was founded in 1886 (all at Oxford). At Cambridge, Girton College was founded in 1872, and Newnham College in 1871. Women students were permitted to study courses, sit examinations, and have their results recorded from 1881, but they were not allowed to take degrees at Oxford and Cambridge until 1920 and 1921, respectively. However, despite these advances in education, their function still served the purpose of delineating masculine and feminine spheres. Women who graduated from college were likely to only become teachers at Board schools (and paid less than their male counterparts!) or at their own alma maters, or were expected to use their intelligence to educate their own children when they married. However, in the Edwardian era, educated ladies found public office open to them and to their liking, and though the vote and a seat in Parliament were denied to them, women could hold office on a lower scale—School Boards, Poor Law Guardians, Inspectors, City Councils, etc.

Nevertheless, education for the lower classes and for women widened and deepened their career horizons. The growth of the Empire lay not merely on the shoulders of its soldiers and seamen, but on its vast network of Civil Service officials, and one can even pinpoint the growth of the middle class not merely to the Industrial Revolution, but to the open examinations that allowed the intelligent son of a grocer to become a clerk in the Civil Service or in the Indian Public Works Department.

The law and medical fields were also wide open to lower class men (and some women), both of which boosted a determined person up the social ladder. The army and navy were still ruled by class—though the navy was less hidebound by privilege than the army—but a young boy of middling birth could enter the ranks as a seaman or private and under the right circumstances, rise to the rank of Admiral or Brigadier by the end of his career.

In the upper class and the aristocracy, the education of girls and boys diverged at quite an early age. Up until a boy was seven or eight, he shared a governess or tutor with his sister, where both were taught the rudiments of reading, writing, and arithmetic. After this, he was sent away to preparatory school, where he was prepared to enter Eton, Harrow, Winchester, or any other top public school at age 12 or 13. His sister, however, was stuck with the governess until she was 16 or 17, and her curriculum consisted only of Hannah More's dreaded "accomplishments".

Some young ladies, depending on the attitude of their parents, read widely on a number of subjects, but the typical lady was much, much less education than her middle-class counterpart. In the meantime, her brother left public school for a college at Oxford or Cambridge at 18, and remained there until about 20 or 21, thereupon his career was decided for him: enter the army or navy (or attend Sandhurst or Dartmouth, where he was study to become a high grade officer), enter the Diplomatic services, or take the Bar.

A young peer was less likely to choose a profession, since the running of his estates and his duties in the House of Lords were his profession.

The passage of the 1870 Education Act (and subsequent acts) leveled the playing field for Edwardian society. The social discrepancies did not disappear, but mobility was easier to achieve. Also, this was the era of women's education, which also played a major role in the growth and spread of the suffragist/ette movement. Those at the top (the gentlemen at least) were still bred to remain at the top and lead the nation, but they no longer had their foot on the necks of the underclass, and from this change sprang the Liberal Party reforms and the Labour Party, as well as the legitimization of trades unions.

The New Woman
The Edwardian era appeared rife with social movements, but none caused as much furor as the "New Woman." From Paris to London to New York to San Francisco, this phenomenon resulted in bitter denunciations, criticism and recriminations that thundered from pulpits to the Houses of Parliament.
The New Woman was a reaction against the long-held notions of femininity and the proper social sphere for women. This reaction was born, ironically, from the very reforms which were to enfranchise men. With schooling compulsory in the

1870s and 1880s, both boys and girls were given at least a basic education, which enabled them to find employment beyond the expectations of their parents' generation.

As a result of the agricultural depression of the 1880s, young men and women, raised on tenant farms, or whose parents were employed by factories, found life insecure and uninspiring. Raised on the abundance of newspapers, periodicals and journals that proliferated in the late Victorian era, the lure of city life was difficult to resist. And so, for the first time, young women left their home for work, not in the traditional pursuit of domestic service, but as a professional.

New technologies spread rapidly across the globe in the second half of the 19th century: the telephone, the telegraph, the elevator, the typewriter, the sewing machine, the cash register, etcetera. With these new technologies came jobs, and these jobs needed bodies to man them. Obviously, men were hired over women, but gradually, women began to make significant inroads in professional employment.

From the working girl of the period—perhaps a saleswoman, a secretary, telephone exchange operator—came the New Woman (or Gibson Girl, as she was characterized in the United States) who was personified by the shirtwaist, tall stiff collar, necktie, and heavy serge skirts she adopted as uniform. Perhaps she would ride her bicycle, which would require the scandalous bloomers.

These "New Women" were not content with their existence as "superfluous" women that characterized the mainstream press's "woman problem"–that is, what to do with the increasing number of women who would never marry? This caused confusion over the gender role of women and led to a "tremendous debate over whether woman's natural role was simply to procreate, or whether women should exercise the same range of choices men had."

These questions and contradictions found a place in the fiction of the period, which was quickly called "New Woman literature."

Playwrights such as Henrik Ibsen and Arthur Wing Pinero wrote popular plays that put modern topics such as venereal disease, prostitution, and the role of marriage in the public eye, while authors like Annie Sophie Cory (Victoria Cross), Sarah Grand, Mona Caird, George Egerton, Ella D'Arcy and Ella Hepworth Dixon put a voice to the trials and tribulations of the New Woman.

Another segment of the New Woman was the "Bachelor Girl." An advice book published during the era characterized the girl-bachelor as a "comfortable creature" and a "clever nest-builder."

More prevalent in American than Europe due to the vaster opportunities for women, the girl-bachelor was most often found in large American cities, sharing a flat or living in a boarding house with other working girls, and working in department stores, millinery shops, couturiers, as a secretary, a clerk, telephone exchange operator, waitress, hat-check girl, and a host of other supporting positions. Far from being old maids, the bachelor girl broke with traditional intersex relations, her financial and social independence putting her outside of the sphere of hearth and home.

Ultimately, the New Woman, the girl-bachelor, challenged and threatened, in the end shattering notions of proper gender roles for women. In reaction to this threat, there poured upon the heads of these women numerous satires in fiction, plays, cartoons and newspaper editorials of the "emancipated woman."

These scornful pieces of media claimed the New Woman had "unsexed" herself and lost the respect of men. They asked in response to "what does she want" with "what does she not want?" She, according to an editorial in the New York Times, "dresses like a man, as far as possible, thereby making herself hideous...the next step will be to wear her hair short and adopt a mustache." She also wants, "to work by man's side and on his level and still be treated with the chivalry due her in her own kingdom—home and society—and any abatement of this treatment produces a storm of indignation and wrath quite beyond the sex she is endeavoring to emulate."

And that's not the worst of the opinions. The retaliation against the New Woman spilled onto the suffrage debate, creating more problems within the movement as not only man pit himself against woman, but woman versus woman as well. Despite this conflict, the New Woman was here to stay, and paved the road for the women of the post-war society.
A key text in the study of the New Woman is Grant Allen's *The Woman Who Did*. Allen was highly sympathetic to the feminist cause and wrote many novels featuring emancipated women. The Penguin anthology, Women Who Did: Stories by Men and Women, 1890-1914, includes Allen's novel and its two rebuttals, *The Woman Who Wouldn't* by Lucas Cleeve and *The Woman Who Didn't* by Victoria Crosse.

Transportation

Four words summed up transportation in Edwardian England: Tube, train, tram, bus, and car, with ocean liners and steamships carrying Britons to faraway places. By the turn of the century, the migration of rural dwellers to cities and towns swelled the boundaries, and with the growth of suburbs, there came a need for cheap and fast travel. The growth of the Empire also created a need to transport troops, tourists, emigrants, and goods to far-flung places around the globe, and the speed and luxury of the steamship was also indicative of the nation's might.

The train, or railway in Brit-speak, has long been considered the symbol of the Industrial Revolution. For much of history, the only way to travel from point A to point B was by horse or by foot, both of which were slow and dependent upon the health of a horse or one's own self. The advent of the railway not only opened the country up to people who until then, expected to live and die in the same village, and travel no further than the nearest town, but it opened up the market for goods and services previously localized to one area.

Aristocratic memoirs of the day mentioned the transport of exotic fruits grown in the hothouse on their country estate to their London townhouse, and shops like Harrods or Peter Robinson or Jay's expanded their empire via mail orders. By the Edwardian era, the train had become commonplace, but the increase in mobility had already changed the way society looked from the bottom up, as the poor and working class were no longer reliant upon what occupations they could find in their village, and tradesmen and farmers were no longer dependent upon middle men.

In a way, being able to pay for train fare, whether it was merely a third class ticket, was indicative of the growing autonomy of the lower orders, as they had freedom from the whims of those in power.

The Tube, or London Underground, had its roots in the 1840s, when it became the "world's oldest subway tunnel." Five decades later saw the opening of the City and South London, and Waterloo and City Railways, in 1890 and 1898 respectively. Oddly enough, the public was rather apathetic to this new mode of transportation, but the tide changed dramatically when in 1900, the Prince of Wales inaugurated the Central London Railway, which ran practically the entire length of London and charged only twopence between any two stations.

Quickly dubbed "The Twopenny Tube" by the Daily Mail, the railway had stations at Shepherd's Bush, Holland Park, Notting Hill Gate, Queen's Road, Lancaster Gate, Marble Arch, Bond Street, Oxford Circus, Tottenham Court Road, British Museum, Chancery Lane, Post Office, and Bank. By the end of 1900, the railway had carried 14,916,922 passengers, and by the death of Edward VII, the line stretched across the entire breadth of London and serviced nearly double that in 1900.

The tram, or tramway, was introduced in the 1850s by an American by the (apt) name of Train, and like all new inventions, were viewed with suspicion and dislike. Train laid his first tracks in Birkenhead (near Liverpool), and tried to introduce the tram to London where their use was met with resistance and classism, as residents of the West End called them the "poor man's street railway." Compounding the unsuitability of the tramway was that it was run by horse until the 1880s. You can imagine the tangle of traffic from horse-drawn carriages, horse-drawn omnibuses, and horse-drawn tramways.

By 1900, after years of experimenting with non-horse power, electricity moved to the forefront. The first electric tram was in Blackpool in 1883, and fittingly, working and lower middle class districts were quick to adopt this mode of travel. The use of the tram never quite reached the well-to-do classes the way the Tube did, but they were very elegant and comfortable in the Edwardian era, being fully upholstered, with curtained windows or fitted with shutters. Because of their strong ties to the lower echelons of the workforce (i.e. white collar professionals), tramways linked suburb to suburb, thereby allowing suburban dwellers ease of travel in the days before the cost of the motorcar decreased. It soon became common for a family to pack a picnic lunch and travel by tram to a seaside resort for short holiday.

The omnibus, later shortened to 'bus, was introduced in the 1820s as a horse-drawn vehicle (of course) intended to convey large numbers of passengers and loosen the congestion in the streets of London and other major cities. Steam and electricity were used in the ensuing decades, but the adoption of the internal combustion engine in the 1890s coincided with the "respectability" of this mode of transport. Until then, ladies were hampered by a host of do's and don'ts for public transportation, and for those without the benefit of the private carriage, it was a wonder any woman was able to travel outside of her house.

Before the introduction of the engine, omnibuses were cramped, dirty, and of varying quality. Passengers were squeezed together in upholstered seats with floors covered with straw, and the closed windows were suffocating. Since the motor 'bus heralded swifter transport, there were now more routes and smaller intervals between 'buses, which in turn lead to bus companies to spruce up their equipment. There were no more windows, the seats were spacious, and it was even respectable for a lady to sit in the top seats.

During the early years of Edward VII's reign, the motorcar was considered a rich man's toy—and the median cost to purchase and keep up this new toy bore this out. The first automobiles were developed in Germany and France, since English law–the Red Flag Act of 1865: "Any vehicle on the public highway, other than a horse-drawn vehicle, must be preceded by a man carrying a red flag in day and a red lantern at night, to warn oncoming traffic of the vehicle behind him."–was influenced by the railway companies, who wished to halt the rising popularity of the steam-cars in the 1850s.

After this act was abolished in 1895, sportsmen and kings took up the vehicle with alacrity, and like the railway did for the working class, the motorcar did for the rich (though while the railway had been an instrument of democracy, the car represented the private ostentation at its most lavish, the final triumph of the haves over the have-nots).

At the end of the Edwardian era, there were several thousand motorcars on the road, though it did not become affordable for any but the most well-to-do until the 1920s (Henry Ford's Model T revolutionized the American automobile market in 1908, but English classism reared its head to keep the market exclusive).

More than anything, the Edwardian era was the age of the Ocean Liner. These sleek and luxurious steamships reached their pinnacle in the 1900s, and were only matched in decadence by the great liners of the 1930s.

The construction of "Ocean Greyhounds" pulled the focus of the ship towards luxury and comfort on the high seas, as well as speed. Now steamships were equipped with staterooms, lounge areas, amenities such as pools and libraries and gyms, and costly decor.

For the top ocean liner companies, such as Cunard, White Star, Hamburg-Amerika, and so on, competed for transatlantic travel (as well as steerage passengers headed from Europe for America) and the Blue Riband—a prize awarded to the fastest steamship across the Atlantic. By the 1910s, the average duration of a crossing was 6-9 days. The Titanic, built by the White Star Line, was amazing, but the true rivalry for supremacy was between Cunard (UK) and Norddeutscher Lloyd (German), who regularly battled for being supremacy in the ocean, until the RMS Mauretania won the Blue Riband in 1909 and held onto that title until 1929.

Chapter 10: The Winds of Change

Politics
The primary focus of Edwardian politics narrowed so tightly to Irish Home Rule, that on the eve of WWI, the topic on the minds of most socialites and politicians was the Third Home Rule Bill. This had been introduced in 1912 and traveled through the same cycle of struggle for passage, rejection by the House of Lords, and multiple readings thereafter that Parliament had seen for the past forty years.

Yet, stronger and more impacting things than merely Irish Home Rule knit the fabric of the political climate. In a scant fourteen years the political landscape was dominated by the debate between Tariff Reform and Protectionism, the menace of trade unionism, the infamous 1906 election, the upsurge of the working class, the suffragist and suffragette movement, the fight to reform of the army and navy, Britain's place in the troubled world of international politics and diplomacy, and the stirrings of the welfare state.

To begin to understand all of this, the major players must be introduced.

The **Conservative Party** traced its origins to a faction, rooted in the 18th century Whig Party that coalesced around William Pitt the Younger. It was originally known as "Independent Whigs", "Friends of Mr. Pitt", or "Pittites," but after Pitt's death the term "Tory" came into use. George Canning first used the term "Conservative" in the 1820s and John Wilson Croker suggested it as a title for the party in the 1830s, but it was Sir Robert Peel who adopted the name and is credited with founding the party.

After the expansion of the franchise, the party widened its appeal under the aegis of Lord Derby and Benjamin Disraeli, who supported the Reform Act of 1867, which enfranchised working class men.

In 1886, the Conservative Party formed an alliance with Lord Hartington (8th Duke of Devonshire) and Sir Joseph Chamberlain's Liberal Unionist Party, which was comprised of the Liberals who opposed their party's support for Irish Home Rule and the combined party held office for all but three of the following twenty years. The Conservatives suffered a large defeat when the party split over the issue of free trade in 1906, and in 1912, the two parties amalgamated into the Unionist party.

Leaders between 1880-1914: Benjamin Disraeli, Marquess of Salisbury, Lord Hartington, Lord Randolph Churchill, Arthur Balfour, Sir Stafford Northcote, Sir Michael Hicks Beach.

The Liberal Party grew out of the Whigs, which had its origins as an aristocratic faction in the reign of Charles II. The Whigs were in favor of reducing the power of the Crown and increasing the power of the Parliament. As early as 1839 Russell had adopted the name Liberal Party, but in reality the party was a loose coalition of Whigs in the House of Lords and Radicals in the Commons.

The formal foundation of the Liberal party is traditionally traced to 1859 and the formation of Palmerston's second government, but it was after Palmerston's death that the Liberal Party reached its zenith. For the next thirty years Gladstone and Liberalism were synonymous. The "Grand Old Man", as he became known, was Prime Minister four times and the powerful flow of his rhetoric dominated British politics even when he was out of office.

The Liberals however, languished during the 1880s and 1890s due to infighting and the coalition of the Conservatives and Liberal Unionists. They rose again after the unpopular Boer War, and were led by Herbert Henry Asquith and David Lloyd George. The Liberals pushed through much legislation in the

1906-1911 period, including the regulation of working hours, national insurance and welfare. It was at this time that a political battle over the so-called People's Budget resulted in the passage of an act ending the power of the House of Lords to block legislation. World War One splintered the group, and it quickly disintegrated after 1918.

Leaders between 1880-1914: William Gladstone, Sir Henry Campbell-Bannerman, David Lloyd George, Herbert Henry Asquith, Winston Churchill (after famously crossing the floor in 1904).

The Liberal Unionist party was created in 1886 from a split in the Liberal Party. Led by Lord Hartington and Joseph Chamberlain, the LU's formed a political alliance with the Conservatives in opposition to Irish Home Rule. The two parties formed a coalition government in 1895 but kept separate political funds and their own party organizations until a complete merger was agreed in May 1912.

The political impact of the Liberal Unionist breakaway marked the end of the long nineteenth century domination by the Liberal party of the British political scene. From 1830 to 1886 the Liberals (the name the Whigs, Radicals and Peelites accepted as their political label after 1859) managed to become almost the party of permanent government with just a couple of Conservative interludes. After 1886 it was the Conservatives who enjoyed this position and they received a huge boost with their alliance with a party of disaffected Liberals.

Leaders between 1880-1914: Marquess of Hartington, Joseph Chamberlain

Commonly called the Irish Party or the Home Rule Party, the Irish Parliamentary Party was formed in 1882 by Charles Stewart Parnell, the leader of the Nationalist Party, replacing the Home Rule League, as official parliamentary party for Irish nationalist Members of Parliament until 1918. The IPP evolved out of the Home Government Association founded by Isaac

Butt after he defected from the Irish Conservative Party in 1870. Its intention was to gain a limited form of freedom from Britain in order to protect and control Irish domestic affairs in the interest of the Protestant landlord class, when William E. Gladstone and his Liberal Party came to power in 1868 under his slogan "Justice for Ireland" and Irish Liberals gained 65 of the 105 Irish seats at Westminster. The party lost its hold when its ardent Catholicism frightened the Protestants, and Butt reorganized the party as the Home Rule League. But no other man is as synonymous with the IPP than Charles Stewart Parnell. Parnell resurrected it in October as the Irish National League (INL).

It combined moderate agrarianism, a Home Rule program with electoral functions, was hierarchical and autocratic in structure with Parnell wielding immense authority and direct parliamentary control. Parliamentary constitutionalism was the future path. The informal alliance between the new, tightly disciplined National League and the Catholic Church was one of the main factors for the revitalization of the national Home Rule cause after 1882.

Parnell saw that the explicit endorsement of Catholicism was of vital importance to the success of this venture. At the end of 1882 the organization already had 232 branches, in 1885 increased to 592 branches. The INL grew to become a formidable political machine built in the traditional political culture of rural Ireland, for it was an alliance of tenant-farmers, shopkeepers and publicans.

The party lost its footing when the scandal of Parnell's relationship with the very married Katherine O'Shea was revealed, and despite the loyalty of his party and friends, Parnell was disgraced. He married Katherine after her divorce, but died soon after. After his death, the Irish Party put pressure on its traditional ally, the Liberal Party, which culminated in a series of Home Rule bills that tore British opinion apart. The outbreak of WWI distracted everyone from the "Irish Question," but Ireland took matters into its own

hands, resulting in the Easter Rising (1916), the war of independence (1919-1921), civil war (1922-1923) and the eventual partition of Ireland into Northern Ireland (Ulster was anti-Home Rule), and the Republic of Ireland.
Leaders between 1880-1914: Charles Stewart Parnell, John Redmond, Justin McCarthy, John Dillon

The Labour Party's origins lie in the late 19th century numeric increase of the urban proletariat and the extension of the franchise to working-class males, when it became apparent that there was a need for a political party to represent the interests and needs of those groups. after the extensions of the franchise in 1867 and 1885, the Liberal Party endorsed some trade-union sponsored candidates.

In addition, several small socialist groups had formed around this time with the intention of linking the movement to political policies. Among these were the Independent Labour Party, the intellectual and largely middle-class Fabian Society, the Social Democratic Federation and the Scottish Labour Party. In the 1892 General Election, held in July, three working men were elected without support from the liberals, Keir Hardie in South West Ham, John Burns in Battersea, and Havelock Wilson in Middlesbrough who faced Liberal opposition. Concurrently Hardie adopted a confrontational style and increasingly emerged as parliamentary spokesman for independent labour.

At the Trade Union Conference meeting in September a meeting of advocates of independent labour organization was called, and chaired by Hardie, an arrangements committee was established and a conference called for the following January. This conference, held in Bradford 14-16 January 1893, was the foundation conference of the Independent Labour Party. The object of the party should be `to secure the collective and communal ownership of the means of production, distribution and exchange'.

The party's program called for a range of reforms, with much more stress on the social – an eight hour working day, provision for sick, disabled aged, widows and orphans and free `unsectarian' education `right up to the universities' – than on the political reforms which were standard in Radical organizations.

In the 1906 election, the party won 29 seats, during their first meeting after the election, the group's MPs decided to adopt the name "The Labour Party". Keir Hardie, who had taken a leading role in getting the party established, was elected as Chairman of the Parliamentary Labour Party. The Fabian Society provided much of the intellectual stimulus for the party.

Leaders between 1880-1914: Keir Hardie, Bruce Glasier, Philip Snowden, Ramsay MacDonald, Frederick William Jowett, William Crawford Anderson

The Irish Question
The "Irish Question" dominated British politics for the majority of the nineteenth century. No other issue tore families, friends, and otherwise friendly political opponents apart than that of Home Rule. The seeds for this conflict were sown long before the nineteenth century, stretching back to the 17th century, when Oliver Cromwell, who detested Roman Catholicism and believed that the Irish could never be trusted, sent his New Model Army and coerce the Irish into obedience.

The army laid siege to the island, the most brutal being that waged on the towns of Wexford and Drogheda, where defenders of the towns were summarily executed. Cromwell also believed the best way to bring Ireland to heel in the long term, was to "export" children from Ireland to the sugar plantations in the West Indies, so that Ireland would suffer from a long term population loss, making it less of a threat to mainland Britain.

Anglo-Irish tensions were further exacerbated by the presence of the "Protestant Ascendancy," or the "Ascendancy," who were comprised of the Protestant English landowners who received large swaths of land from the Crown confiscated from Irish landowners after a series of unsuccessful revolts against English rule. English soldiers and traders became the new ruling class, as its richer members were elevated to the Irish House of Lords, and eventually controlled the Irish House of Commons. This process was facilitated and formalized in the legal system after 1691 by the passing of various Penal Laws, which discriminated against Irish Catholics and non-Anglican Protestants deemed "Dissenters."

Though the Ascendancy lost much of its overt political and social clout by the early 19th century, the "abolition of the Irish parliament was followed by economic decline in Ireland, and widespread emigration from among the ruling class to the new center of power in London, which increased the number of absentee landlords." The Potato Famine of 1848-1852 exposed the vulnerability of Irish tenant farmers, and as a consequence, the British Parliament was moved to pass a number of acts to bolster the Irish economy. But these belated Acts did little to counteract the centuries of absentee landlord abuses, nor the history of British oppression.

The life of an Irish tenant farmer was difficult. Land prices in Ireland were high—sometimes 80-100% higher than in England—and those who leased land from an absentee landlord rented out small parcels to those who paid to farm it. Each estate leased out was divided into the smallest possible parcels of land and many families who worked the land had only half-an-acre to live on.

There were no rules controlling the work of those who had leased land from absentee landlords, and this lack of rules worked in conjunction with the Royal Irish Constabulary who, with the Army, enforced evictions if needed. As such, there were three systems in place which forced Irish farmers into the endless cycle of debt:

Rundale: a system whereby land rented to a person or persons was scattered throughout an estate. Therefore, it was very time consuming to travel to each parcel of land. The argument given for using this system was that everyone got a chance of getting at least some good land to farm. One man in Donegal had 42 pieces of land throughout one managed estate.

Hanging Gale: a system whereby a new tenant was allowed to delay his payment of rent for 6 to 8 months from the start of renting the land. Therefore, he was permanently in debt and had no security.

Conacre: a system whereby the landlord/manager prepared the land and then the tenant moved in. The tenant was then allowed to pay part of his rent using the crops he had grown. If there was a bad harvest, then he had no crops to pay part of his rent. Therefore, he was gambling that he would get a good harvest. In 1845 to 1847, this system was ripe for a disaster.

Dissent spilled over in the 1840s and 1850s with the rise of the Young Ireland party. They believed the only solution for Ireland was complete independence: Home Rule. After a failed attack on the government, Young Ireland's most prominent leaders, James Stephens and John O'Mahony, fled for Paris. O'Mahoney later found his way to America where he stirred up the ire of Irish-Americans to create the Fenian Brotherhood. The Fenians planned a number of rebellions and uprisings, and though initially their causes garnered much sympathy, after December 1867, when several Londoners were killed when a bomb planted by the Fenians exploded at Clerkenwell Prison, there came a wave of intense anti-Irish feeling in London and elsewhere in England.

Prior to his taking up the cudgel for Home Rule, William Ewart Gladstone's political career was somewhat distinguished but mostly ordinary. In 1867, Lord Russell retired and Gladstone became a leader of the Liberal Party, shortly thereafter becoming Prime Minister, where he remained in the office until 1874.

In the 1860s and 1870s, Gladstonian Liberalism was "characterized by a number of policies intended to improve individual liberty and loosen political and economic restraints. First was the minimization of public expenditure on the premise that the economy and society were best helped by allowing people to spend as they saw fit. Secondly, his foreign policy aimed at promoting peace to help reduce expenditures and taxation and enhance trade. Thirdly, laws that prevented people from acting freely to improve themselves were reformed."

During Gladstone's rise, there also arose Ireland's most intelligent and charismatic leader, one whom many on both sides of the political spectrum admitted could have swayed the tide of Home Rule: Charles Stewart Parnell. Born into the gentry and, surprisingly, of American stock via his mother, he rose swiftly through the ranks of politics, gaining fame during the 1870s when he refuted the claims that Fenians had been behind the murders in Manchester.

His defense gained him the attention of the Irish Republican Brotherhood (IRB), a physical force Irish organization that had staged the rebellion in 1867, and Parnell began to cultivate Fenians from America and Britain. By the 1880s, Parnell had become the face of Irish Nationalism, and so popular was he that during his tour of Toronto, an associate dubbed him the "uncrowned king of Ireland."

By the time of Gladstone's Second and Third Ministries, he was aligned with the pro-Home Rule movement. Gladstone, impressed by Parnell, had become personally committed to granting Irish home rule in 1885. With his famous three-hour Irish Home Rule speech Gladstone sought to convince Parliament to "pass the Irish Government Bill 1886, and grant Home Rule to Ireland in honor rather than being compelled to do so one day in humiliation."

The bill was defeated in the Commons by 30 votes. The split the Liberal (Whig) Party led to the founding of the Liberal

Unionists by Lord Hartington (later the Duke of Devonshire, whose brother was murdered by Irish nationalists at Phoenix Park in 1886) and Joseph Chamberlain, who then formed a political alliance with the Conservatives in opposition to Irish Home Rule.

From then on, the "Irish Question" was fought bitterly in the House of Commons, and politicians were not afraid to resort to various deceptions such as forgeries, bribes, dissenting anonymous pamphlets, etc in support or in opposition. One of these backdoor deals is rumored to have resulted in the sudden petition for divorce by Captain O'Shea, the husband of Parnell's longtime love, Katherine, with whom he had three children.

The divorce scandal stunted Parnell's political career, and though he remained popular, his reputation was forever tarnished and he died in 1891. The fight for Home Rule marched on, and prior to the Great War, two more Home Rule bills were introduced in 1892 and 1914, only to experience a crushing defeat (though the 1914 bill was interrupted by WWI and the Easter Rising). Though the issue of Home Rule was finally settled violently and bloodily, it cast a pall over British politics and was the first sign of a weakness in the armor that was the British Empire.

The Suffrage Movement
The militant suffrage movement in Great Britain began as a Pankhurst family enterprise that, from 1903 to 1905 remained focused around Manchester, until the general election of 1905 brought matters to a head. Prior to the Pankhursts, the fight for women's suffrage in Britain was a relatively tame one. In the mid 1860s, a group of women, all pursuing a career in either medicine or education, formed a discussion group dubbed the "Kensington Society".

Their initial reasons for forming the group had little to do with suffrage; the seven founding ladies merely wished for a society

of like-minded women of independent means and an interest in fields not normally associated with the female sex.
It wasn't until the topic of suffrage was raised that the Kensington Society discovered their mutual dismay. In reaction, they drafted a petition asking parliament to extend to vote to women. Presenting the petition to Henry Fawcett and John Stuart Mill, a pair of MPs known for their sympathy towards women's suffrage, the Kensington Society saw their petition almost immediately shot down in Parliament. V

astly disappointed with the action, they formed the London Society for Women's Suffrage. Soon thereafter, many cities in Britain found themselves hosts to similar societies.
In 1887, seventeen of these groups formed the National Union of Women's Suffrage Societies, or NUWSS. Under the presidencies of Lydia Becker and Millicent Fawcett, the society raised awareness of the cause by holding meetings, holding marches, printing pamphlets and newsletters, and writing politicians and petitions.

NUWSS also lent support to Josephine Butler's campaign against white slavery as well as Clementia Black's attempts to force the government to protect low-paid women workers. Inoffensive, efficient and ladylike, NUWSS attracted support from all walks of life—including a good number of men.

The cause chugged along in this manner until the Manchester group splintered, and the women, led by Christabel Pankhurst, grew fed up with the constitutional methods NUWSS favored. The Women's Social & Political Union (WSPU) was born.
A far cry from the genteel group from whence they came, the WSPU immediately showed its difference in the fact that it attracted women from the working and middle-classes—women who were less inhibited by the traditional trappings of "ladyhood".

Though at first fearing the stance the WSPU took would harm the cause, the NUWSS admired their courage and refused to speak out against them. However, by 1905 public interest in women's suffrage had waned, and the WSPU made a decision that would forever change the face of the suffragist movement. Christabel Pankhurst and Annie Kenny threw down the gauntlet by interrupting Sir Edward Grey's speech during a Liberal Party meeting with the cry of "Will the Liberal Government give votes to women?".

The women were soon after charged with assault and arrested. Christabel and Annie then proceeded to shock the world when, after refusing to pay the five shilling fine, they were thrown in jail. Never before had English suffragists resorted to violence to support the cause and newspapers were quick to pounce on this new movement, with the Daily Mail nicknaming the followers of militancy "suffragettes". Far from decrying this derogatory term, the WSPU adopted it with pleasure since the term separated them from the moderate actions of the NUWSS.

The WSPU moved their headquarters from Manchester to London, by 1908 the suffragettes had launched an all-out war for the cause, targeting those MPs notoriously anti-suffrage like Prime Minister H.H. Asquith and Winston Churchill. The suffragettes marched through London, interrupted speeches, assaulted policemen attempting to arrest them, chained themselves to fences, sent letter bombs and damaged property–the most infamous being their destruction of the windows of department stores and shops in Bond Street. Viewed as unfeminine since many of the women were unmarried and had careers instead of housework, the Establishment were at a loss as to how to deal with suffragettes.

They baffled the common perceptions of Victorian womanhood, and once they were released from jail, the suffragettes merely went out and repeated the same misdemeanors. By using this loophole in the justice system, the suffragettes increased their militant campaigns, including a devastating arson campaign during which attempts were made to burn the houses of anti-suffrage MPs, railway stations, golf courses, cricket fields and racecourse stands. When the jailed suffragettes went on hunger-strikes while incarcerated, the government passed the "Cat and Mouse Act" in 1913: if a suffragette went on a hunger strike, once ill she would be released from prison and re-arrested when well again.

By the summer of 1914, the militant campaign was exhausted by the imprisonment, exile or poor health of the WSPU's leading members (Christabel had fled to Paris in 1912 to escape arrest), and the splits within the WSPU, and the number of active members able to continue the violence was now very small. Naturally, WWI put a damper on the suffrage campaign, and both the WSPU and NUWSS focused their energies on the war effort, using their platforms to drum up support for the troops.

But ever antagonistic to the end, the WSPU took patriotism to their breast as much as they did suffrage, using their newspaper to attack those in power whom they saw as pacifists or communists. In the end, married women over the age of 30 were granted the vote in 1918, and ten years later the vote was given on equal terms as men (age 21).

Trade Unions, Working Class Power & Social Welfare
The Education Act of 1870 educated the working class, and the Third Reform Act of 1884 empowered them (well, the men at least). From this educated and enfranchised mass came trade unions. Unions had been brutally suppressed until the 1820s, but in the 1880s, new unions were militant, led by men with a socialist bent, recruited semi-skilled and unskilled labor as opposed to just skilled trades, and used their mobility to spread their ideas.

They were also unafraid to go on strike, and there were three major disputes between 1894 and 1898 (the Scottish Coal Miners' in 1894, the Engineers' in 1897-98, and the South Wales Coal Miners' in 1898).

In 1901, the position of the trade unions were challenged when the Taff Vale Railway Company "successfully sued the Amalgamated Society of Railway Servants, a trades union, for damages due to losses accrued during a strike." The Company won £23,000 in damages, which proved that trade unions were not immune to the damages caused by its members, but this lawsuit only infuriated the working classes and alienated them from the Conservative Party who set up a Royal Commission in 1906 merely to discuss the situation.

The Conservatives were in for an extremely rude awakening that year, for during the General Election, they lost over half their seats in the House of Commons, the Liberals—under Campbell-Bannerman—gained a clear majority, and the Labour Party considerably increased its seats.

This election also saw the downfall of the Liberal Unionist party, who experienced their own split between the moderate LU's and the more radical members allied with Joseph Chamberlain, over the debate between Free Trade vs. Tariff Reform. Chamberlain had always been strongly pro-Empire, and he saw the installment of tariffs on imported goods and subsidies on exported goods as a way to bind the Empire more tightly together and help Britain maintain its power in the face of German and American industrialization and wealth.

This sounded good on paper, but for the working classes, this was a repeat of the Corn Laws of 1815-1846 (which protected homegrown grains and cereals from competition against imported grains and cereals, but ultimately led to high prices and low wages).

Chamberlain's political career reached its zenith between 1903 and 1904, when he became the face of Tariff Reform, the cause for which he stumped across England giving rousing speeches to sway electors to his side. Unfortunately, the winds of change were against him, and the Liberal Unionist Party collapsed in the months leading up to the 1906 General Election. The Pro-Tariff Reform Liberal Unionists and Conservatives in

Chamberlain's hometown of Birmingham remained triumphant, but everyone else lost their seats or retreated to the Liberal or Conservative Parties from whence they came. The Prime Minister Sir Henry Campbell-Bannerman died two years after he lead the Liberal Party to its victory and was replaced by his Chancellor of the Exchequer (what would be known as the Secretary of the Treasury in the US), Herbert Henry Asquith.

Now the face of British politics had definitely changed for Asquith, and his Chancellor of the Exchequer, David Lloyd George, were both staunchly upper-middle class, non-Anglican (Asquith was raised a Congregationalist, Lloyd George a Nonconformist), and were not land owners—three attributes which placed them firmly outside of the traditional political mold. They were also progressive, though Lloyd George more so than Asquith, and with the equally fiery Winston Churchill, launched a campaign to reform British society.

Topics mentioned before, such as women's suffrage, workmen's compensation, trade unionism, old age pensions, and sweated labor, to say nothing of Home Rule, unemployment, and child welfare, aroused heated debates from the Palace of Westminster to social and political gatherings across the nation. Times were changing swiftly and violently, but no act of social reform aroused as much controversy and firestorm as the People's Budget of 1909.

The People's Budget was the brainchild of David Lloyd George and was championed by his ally, Winston Churchill, who was accused of being a traitor to his class. Lloyd George, a Welsh politician who gained fame by his vehement opposition to the Second Boer War, made social reform the linchpin of his personal political platform. Though it could be said that the Liberal Party adopted a measure of socialistic platforms to keep the Conservative Party in check, and to stem the rise of the Labour Party, Edwardian society was changing, and politicians were kicked into the twentieth century, whether they liked it or not.

After the Liberals introduced old age pensions for the sick and infirm, Lloyd George shocked both sides of the political spectrum with the budget he revealed on April 29, 1909, which proposed taxes on luxuries, liquor, tobacco, incomes, and land, and an increase in death duties (introduced in 1894) and duties on undeveloped land and minerals, a levy on unearned increment, and a supertax on incomes above £5000 (6d. on the pound).

This influx of taxes would support such programs as pensions, unemployment insurance, health insurance, free school meals for children, etc, and the costs of building the dreadnoughts the Royal Navy claimed it needed to shore up defenses against Germany.

Also causing controversy was the reform of the Army under the Secretary of State for War, Richard Haldane. The physical conditions of recruits during the Boer War exposed the shameful state in which poor and working class people lived. These young men who rushed to enlist were puny, underfed, and in no shape to fight Boers under the hot South African sun. But the British Army was incredibly slow to adapt and very resistant to change, and when the war ended, they considered the matter closed.

Haldane didn't, and when he was appointed Secretary of State during the Liberal landslide, he was determined to whip the Army into shape. The Territorial and Reserve Forces Act of 1907 enabled him to launch his reform: a Territorial Force and a Reserve Army—both of which formed the foundation of the British Expeditionary Forces sent to France in WWI.

This was too much for the traditional Establishment to handle, but their successes in establishing a Territorial Army, making sweated labor illegal, and Old Age Pensions made them sure of their budget, which galvanized the Liberal Party to action. They fought for the Finance Bill throughout the summer, but a blow was struck when the House of Lords vetoed the budget, and the tug-of-war resulted in another General Election in

January 1910. A greater blow was struck to the House of Lords, who, though they passed the budget April 29, 1910, experienced their first real challenge of power.
So great was the battle for the People's Budget, Liberal politicians threatened to make King Edward (and after his death in May, King George) ennoble Liberal MPs so they could then sit in the House of Lords and pass the bill.

This constitutional crisis did not come to pass, but 1911 saw the passing of a Parliament Act which "prevented the Lords from vetoing any public legislation that originated in and had been approved by the Commons, and imposed a maximum legislative delay of one month for "money bills" (those dealing with taxation) and two years for other types of bill."

Society was rent in two as much by this crisis as by Irish Home Rule, and the thirty odd years of "peace" between the major political parties (from which sprang The Souls, who were adamant that everyone bridge the gap between their political beliefs in order to enjoy one another's company) were over. In the four years between Edward VII's death and the outbreak of WWI, England was far, far from the bucolic "long Edwardian summer" so many post-war memoirs harkened back to with longing. In fact, much of the period was marked by strife, estrangement, and violence, as the people pushed against the marginalization created in the Nineteenth century and were determined to bring the nation into the Twentieth.

British Diplomacy and the Road to the Great War
When in 1902, Britain raised its head from its "splendid isolation" to realize it had no allies, its enemies and neutral peers had long since formed alliances and treaties that crisscrossed across Europe. One can see the thread tying various countries together in the mad declarations of war in the summer of 1914 (Austria-Hungary on Serbia, Russia on Austria-Hungary, Germany on Russia, France on Germany, etc), and Britain herself was pulled into the melee by a treaty with Belgium from the 1830s.

In 1873 Russia, Germany, and Austria-Hungary signed a pact called the "League of the Three Emperors." Since the three dominated a large swath of land and people, it was considered imperative that they look out for one another. Yet, the Emperors (Tsar Alexander II, Franz Josef, and Wilhelm I)—and Bismarck—failed to take into account their individual agendas.

Russia considered the Balkan region, long under Ottoman reign, its sister since both Russia and the Balkans were made up of predominantly Slavic peoples. Austria-Hungary, however, considered the Balkans, who gave the landlocked empire warm water and regular ports and were due south to Austria and Hungary, their own.

When the Ottoman Empire collapsed in 1878 and its possessions parceled out between the leading Powers, the tension between Russia and Austria-Hungary simmered until the alliance finally broke for good in 1887. Germany and Austria-Hungary had since signed their own secret Dual Alliance, and in 1882, Italy surreptitiously joined them to form the Triple Alliance. Bismarck could not allow Russia to go and align itself with France, and he badgered Russia into a secret treaty known as the "Reinsurance Treaty" in 1887, wherein Germany promised to stay out of any conflict between Russia and Austria-Hungary.

Unfortunately, Bismarck's best laid plans went awry when Wilhelm II ascended to the throne of the German Empire after his father's premature death after eight months of rule in 1888. The arrogant and impetuous young Kaiser decided to rid himself of anything and anyone associated with his father and grandfather's reigns, and meddle in foreign affairs himself. With the Iron Chancellor dropped, the secret treaty with Russia was as well, and Bismarck's worst fears came true with Russia publicly aligned itself with France in 1892.

In the meantime, Britain felt threatened on all sides: by her traditional enemy France, by Russia, whom they feared would attempt to take India from them (this "cold war" between Russia and Britain was played out in Central Asia [Afghanistan, Persia, Turkestan, etc] and was known as the Great Game), and by the rapidly-industrialized and militarized Germany, whom they mistrusted. Britain and France nearly came to blows in 1898 with the Fashoda Incident, when a French expedition in East Africa sought to take control of the Nile River and expel Britain from Egypt.

The frantic diplomats of both nations and the show of Britain's might only averted battle when it sent a flotilla of gunboats to Fashoda. As a result of this humiliation, French opinion of Britain greatly soured, and when the British declared the Second Boer War in 1899, the press in all of its enemy nations were brutal.

Britain's first friend was Japan, with whom they admittedly had little in common other than a opposition to Russian expansion in the East. The Anglo-Japanese Alliance was signed in January 1902, and in March a mutual pact was signed by France and Russia, which ultimately had the effect of keeping France out of the Russo-Japanese War of 1904-05, since that would have embroiled the French in a war with Britain. Meanwhile, this alliance had the positive affect of bringing a bit of Japan to England and a bit of England to Japan.

After this first step at ending its diplomatic isolation, it seemed natural than Britain would align itself with Germany. After all, the Kaiser was Queen Victoria's grandson and King Edward VII's nephew, and the cultural exchange between the two nations were actually quite strong. Many of Britain's top politicians assumed a German treaty would be the natural conclusion, but the King had other ideas.

Edward had loved France since he was a little boy. When the Emperor Louis-Napoleon and his lovely wife Eugenie visited England in the 1850s, the little Prince of Wales was seduced by French manners, French language, French culture, and best of all, French beauties (the perfumed and beautifully-dressed ladies in the Empress's retinue). As an adult, he was as much at home in French salons and French racetracks as he was in English drawing rooms and English race courses, and the French aristocracy were so mad about him, many became ardent Anglophiles, even going so far as to begin the custom of having afternoon tea.

Now as King he was determined to bring the two nations he loved best together, and in the spring of 1904, France and Britain signed the Entente Cordiale, thus ending almost a thousand years of enmity between them, and signaling to Germany that Britain would never be their ally.

With the Entente, France and Britain let bygones be bygones in the squabble for North Africa, but the world experienced a further shock when Britain and Russia finally laid down the weapons in their cold war and signed the Anglo-Russian Entente in 1907, thereby establishing once and for all the boundaries between India and Central Asia.

In the meantime, Germany began to meddle in the affairs of the weak Ottoman Empire, and Austria-Hungary's abrupt annexation of Bosnia-Herzegovina in 1908 nearly blew the fuse seething in the Balkans.

With the former, Germany descended upon the "Sick Man of Europe" with its engineers and bankers, and promises of loans, support, and industrialization, and with the latter, Austria had practically pounced when the other nations weren't looking. This move outraged the Ottomans, Russia and the Balkan peoples, which nearly upset German's hold over the Ottoman Empire, since remember, Austria-Hungary was their ally.

However, when Italy defeated the Ottomans in 1912, the Balkan nations realized how weak the Ottoman Empire was, and how hesitant the European powers were to meddle in their affairs, and promptly declared war. 1912 and 1913 saw the

Ottoman Empire felled for good after five hundred years of rule in Eastern Europe, the Middle East, and North Africa, and the establishment of independent nations in the Balkan Peninsula (Albania, Serbia, Macedonia, and Bulgaria).

France and Germany's own bitter rivalry spilled over during this time as well, with two crises over the status of Morocco. As one of the last independent countries in Africa and situated beside France's colonial possessions in North Africa, it was a given that the French would want to add Morocco to its possessions. Germany, however, was determined to meddle, and in 1906, the Kaiser sailed away to Morocco to offer the Sultan his support in maintaining the country's independence.

The dispute was calmed by a conference of the world powers and France was announced the natural protector of Morocco, but it reared its head again in 1911, when the Kaiser sent a gunboat to the port of Agadir during a rebellion against the Sultan. The result of this crisis was to allow France to annex Morocco, thereby ending its independence, in exchange for a piece of France's territory in the Congo.

All of these conflicts, practically one after another, served only to draw particular nations further together against other nations, and now we see the world on the edge of war. But Britain remained blind to the implications of this, distracted as it was by its own domestic troubles, and when Austria declared war on Serbia in July of 1914, many assumed the war would be localized and brief, or even calmed by yet another conference and treaty. Unfortunately for them, the web of alliances and agendas that entangled the Concert of Europe had been spun too deep for too long, and it took a major war to force it apart.

Conclusion
With the declarations of War in August of 1914, the epoch alternately known as the Edwardian age, La Belle Epoque, or more ominously, fin de siècle, ended with—literally—a bang. Nearly one hundred years after its conclusion, WWI appears a preventable tragedy, or a baffling piece of history, and is

mourned for the loss of "innocence" with which the long, sunny summers bathed the Edwardians.

In reality, though war was unexpected, it was largely inevitable when it was declared the world seemed to heave a sigh of relief and shrug its shoulders in anticipation of relieving the incredible tension built up between the Powers and its satellites stretching back to the unification of Germany.

And yet, society was largely ignorant of the impending conflict. The social seasons of Paris, London, New York, et al remained brilliant, and the only turmoil worrying England was domestic: militant suffragettes (though force-feedings and the "Cat and Mouse Act" forced leaders of the movement to flee imprisonment), the Irish Question, and "serious industrial unrest and an enormous increase in trade union membership, which affected all industries."

Not even the rising nationalism within the British Empire (notably in India) failed to alarm the English. Mostly, the topic of war remained unfathomable because so many believed it utterly impossible in the face of so many exciting technological advances, advances that proved the might and intelligence of mankind over its formerly primitive state (ironically, technology hastened the war and increased its deadliness— dreadnoughts, chemicals [mustard gas], submarines, airplanes, machine guns, etc). Besides, war was simply out of date!

Many memoirs and diaries published in the aftermath of WWI chronicled the end of their relatively peaceful era, and most expressed the contentment, confusion and disbelief of the weeks leading up to the declaration of war. That summer, the summer of 1914 was marked for its warmth and fineness, the best in living memory; the "thunderbolt, when it fell, descended from a cloudless sky."

One morning in June, 1914, Desmond Chapman-Huston "motored in Tisbury to get petrol or something. The newspapers had not arrived before I left. As the tank was being filled I idly noted a poster which said: 'Murder of an Austrian Archduke.' While Germany invaded Belgium, leaving Britain to deal with an ultimatum expiring midnight on August 3rd, "Monday, August 1st, the party broke up, some to go to Cowes for Cowes Week, I to go to Fleet to my mother for a few days...I left Fleet after luncheon; the train was crowded with Naval and Military Reservists recalled to their units by telegram...Soldiers were everywhere!"

Wilfrid Scawen Blunt's diary offers a succinct, yet anxious picture of this tumultuous time:

30th June. — There has been another assassination, this time of the heir of the Austrian Emperor. I do not quite know how it affects the political situation.

27th July. — To-day's papers are sensational. War seems to have begun on the Danube, and there has been rioting in Dublin, with firing on the mob and a bayonet charge, with two or three people killed and many wounded. This will bring things to a head and oblige Asquith to allow the arming of the National Volunteers if he does not throw up his cards and resign. This is an astonishing show of weakness and mismanagement. I see the Labour members are threatening a revolt from Asquith and a hundred Liberals as well if he does not withdraw the Amendment Bill and keep the Army in order.
30th July. — The crisis is worse than ever, with panic on all the Stock Exchanges of Europe and our own. Advantage is being taken of it to defer any settlement of the Irish question on the ground that all parties are of one patriotic mind, Irish as well as English, towards events abroad. This is of course absurd, but so long as the King puts his signature to the Home Rule Bill, the rest will not matter. The first shots have been fired in Servia.

31st July. — The *Times* to-day has a special article in largest print recommending England to go to war in aid of France against Germany, but I do not believe in any such folly.

Belgrade has been bombarded, and it is all but certain now there will be general European war, but not for us. Belloc and I differ in this. He is convinced that France is stronger than Germany. I am not. He talks of Germany as calling out to our Foreign Office to mediate. I believe Germany means war, and is rejecting Grey's foolish intervention.

1st Aug. — There is a general panic, the London Stock Exchange closed, and the Bank rate raised to 8 per cent. Germany has sent ultimatums both to Russia and to France; general war is certain, but the *Times* has a letter from Norman Angell in large print to-day contradictory of its yesterday's article. The *Nation* and all the Liberal papers denounce the idea of war, and I cannot believe we shall be such fools as to take part in it if we are not attacked. Italy is proclaiming neutrality; we shall do the same.

3rd Aug. — Things are marching fast. The Germans have begun their campaign against France by seizing Luxembourg, and seem to be already in Belgium. The news of this they say reached the Cabinet while it was sitting last evening (the second in the day, and that Sunday), and united all the Ministers to resolve, it is not said what. The naval reserves are being called out.

4th Aug. — Grey's declaration turns out to be not quite what the evening papers said. It is evidently a compromise between the two opinions in the Cabinet. It denies the obligation to assist France against Germany, except to the extent of preventing bombardment by sea of the French seaboard in the Channel, but it affirms the duty of defending Belgian neutrality, and will lead us farther than the peace division think, for it must be remembered that all the action will be left in Grey's hands at the Foreign Office, and in Winston's at the Admiralty, and it will be easy for them to manipulate accidents into a case of necessity for despatching a land force to Antwerp. So we are not out of the wood yet. On the contrary, the British Army has been formally mobilised, and the reservists called to the colours. Our local policeman called today to inquire how many horses I could put up in my barns. Both Burrell and Leconfield have had a number of horses earmarked for service, Leconfield as many as forty. I said I could put up twenty under cover, but everything connected with soldiering is hateful to me. There is talk of a British ultimatum to Germany, demanding an answer about the neutrality of Belgium being respected.

5th Aug. — The thing has been decided faster than we imagined. Yesterday Asquith announced in the Commons that Grey had sent his ultimatum to Berlin about Belgian neutrality, and had received an unsatisfactory answer, and to-day the morning papers publish "British Declaration of War against Germany."

The response to this was largely patriotic. Men young and old rushed to be conscripted, their heads filled with the tales of valor and honor of warriors in the past. Public schools bred young men willing to fight for England against the tyranny of the "Hun", for "France to be saved, Belgium righted, freedom and civilization re-won, a sour, soiled, crooked old world to be rid of bullies and crooks and reclaimed for straightness, decency, good-nature, the ways of common men dealing with common men."

The early War poems of Kipling, Brooke, and Grenfell, expressed the ecstatic outlook of aristocratic men, which, along with reassurances that the war would be "over by Christmas" whipped up enthusiasm for enlistment. What we–and what they very quickly realized–know now is that the battle was a long, slow, and arduous slaughter, after which the vestiges of the 19th century were shelled, torpedoed, and hammered until a new society, a 20th century society, emerged from the ashes. Yet, when we continue to look at the post-WWI era, the roots of modernism stand strong in the late 19th and early 20th centuries, waiting for the right spark to bring them to fruition.

RESOURCES

Books
The 1900s Lady by Kate Caffrey
1913: The Defiant Swan Song by Virginia Cowles
American Jennie: The Remarkable Life of Lady Randolph Churchill by Anne Sebba
Autobiography by Margot Asquith
The Asquith Parliament (1906-1909) by Charles Thomas King
The Age of Extravagance: An Edwardian Reader by Mary Elisabeth Edes, Dudley Frasier and James Laver
The Age of Upheaval: Edwardian politics 1899-1914 by David Brooks
Baedekers' Guidebooks
The Balfourian Parliament, 1900-1905 by Sir Henry William Lucy
Behind the Wheel: The Magic and Manners of early motoring by Lord Montagu of Beaulieu
The Big Shots: Edwardian Shooting Parties by Jonathan Garnier Ruffer
British Social Politics by Carlton Hayes
Book of Household Management by Mrs. Beeton
The Book of Parliament by Michael MacDonagh
Carriages at Eleven: The Story of the Edwardian Theatre by W. Macqueen-Pope
A Diary of the Salisbury Parliament, 1886-1892 by Sir Henry William Lucy
A Diary of the Unionist parliament: 1895-1900 by Sir Henry William Lucy
A Diary of the Home rule Parliament, 1892-1895 by Sir Henry William Lucy
The Decline and Fall of the British Aristocracy by David Cannadine
The Deluge: British Society and the First World War by Arthur Marwick
Dreadnought by Robert K. Massie
The English Country House Party by Phyllida Barstow

Education of Girls and Women in Great Britain by C.S. Bremner
Edward and the Edwardians by Philippe Jullian
Edwardian England 1901 - 1914 by Simon Nowell-Smith
Edwardian Interiors: Inside the Homes of the Poor, the Average, and the Wealthy by Alastair Service
The Edwardian Farm by Jonathan Brown
The Edwardian Lady by Susan Tweedsmuir
Edwardian Life and Leisure by Ronald Pearsall
Edwardian Promenade by James Laver
The Edwardian Woman by Duncan Crow
The Edwardians by J. B. Priestley
The Edwardians by Vita Sackville-West
The Edwardians: the Remaking of British Society by Paul Richard Thompson
Emmeline Pankhurst: A Biography by June Purvis
Escoffier: The Complete Guide to the Art of Modern Cookery by H. L. Cracknell and R. J. Kaufmann
The Fast Set: The World of Edwardian Racing by George Plumptre
Food in History by Reay Tannahill
Forgotten Elegance: The Art, Artifacts, and Peculiar History of Victorian and
Edwardian Entertaining in America by Wendell Schollander and Wes Schollander
Gay Monarch: The Life and Pleasures of Edward VII by Virginia Cowles
Girls Growing up in late Victorian and Edwardian England by Carol Dyhouse
Gladstone: A Biography by Roy Jenkins
The Gladstone Parliament 1880-1885 by Sir Henry William Lucy
The Glitter and the Gold by Consuelo Vanderbilt Balsan
The Great Illusion 1900-1914 by Oron J. Hale
The Guns of August by Barbara Tuchman
Handbook of Home rule, Being Articles on the Irish Question by James Bryce
High Society: The English Social Elite, 1880-1914 by Pamela Horn

The History of the Art of Table setting by Claudia Quigley Murphy
Home Life in America by Katherine Graves Busbey
Home Rule: An Irish history, 1800-2000 by Alvin Jackson
Homes of the Passing Show by Various Authors
The House of Lords Question by Andrew Reid, Philip Stanhope, and Robert Collier Monkswell
How We are Governed: Guide for the Stranger to the Houses of Parliament by Howard Vincent
Inside the Victorian Home: A Portrait of Domestic Life in Victorian England by Judith Flanders
The IRB: The Irish Republican Brotherhood, from the Land League to Sinn Fein by Owen Mcgee
Ladies of the Manor by Pamela Horn
The Laurel and the Ivy: The Story of Charles Stewart Parnell and Irish Nationalism by Robert Kee
Later Peeps at Parliament Taken from Behind the Speaker's Chair by Sir Henry William Lucy
Life's Ebb and Flow by Frances, Countess of Warwick
Living London Vols 1-3 Edited by George Sims
London of To-Day, Vols 1888-1902 by Charles Eyre Pascoe
The London Season by Louis T. Stanley
Manor House: Life in an Edwardian Country House by Juliet Gardiner
The Marlborough House Set by Anita Leslie
To Marry an English Lord by Carol McD. Wallace
Mr. Lloyd George by E. T. Raymond
My Diaries, v.2, by Wilfrid Scawen Blunt
The New Girl: Girls' Culture in England, 1880-1915 by Sally Mitchell
A New Woman Reader by Carolyn Christensen Nelson
The Opulent Eye: Late Victorian and Edwardian Taste in Interior Design by Nicholas Cooper
Origins of the First World War by Gordon Martel
Out in Noonday Sun by Valerie Pakenham
Peeps at Parliament: Taken from Behind the Speaker's Chair by Sir Henry William Lucy
The Public School Phenomenon, 597–1977 by Jonathan Gathorne-Hardy

The Pursuit of Pleasure by Keith Middlemas
Political Woman by Melville Currell
Queen Alexandra by Georgina Battiscombe
The Rainbow Comes and Goes by Lady Diana Cooper
Remember and Be Glad by Lady Cynthia Asquith
The Renaissance of Girls' Education in England: A Record of Fifty Years' Progress by Alice Zimmern
The Rise and Fall of the Victorian Servant by Pamela Horn
The Rise of the Democracy by Joseph Clayton
Rosa Lewis: An Exceptional Edwardian by Anthony Masters
Secret Service by Sir George Aston
Seventy Years Young by Countess Fingall
Scenes of Edwardian life by Charles Petrie
Social Calendar by Anna Sproule
Social Transformations of the Victorian Age by T.H.S. Escott
Society in the New Reign by T.H.S. Escott
The Story of Secret Service by Richard Wilmer Rowan
The Sway of the Grand Saloon: A Social History of the North Atlantic by John Malcolm Brinnin
Table Service by Lucy Grace Allen
Toynbee Hall and the English Settlement Movement by Werner Picht
Tube, Train, Tram, and Car: Or Up-To-Date Locomotion by Arthur Henry Beavan
The Up-to-date Waitress by Janet McKenzie Hill
The Victorian and Edwardian Schoolchild by Pamela Horn
Women, Marriage, and Politics, 1860-1914 by Pat Jalland
A Word to Women by Charlotte Eliza Humphry

Periodicals, Newspapers & Magazines
The Bystander
The Illustrated London News
The Graphic
The Lady's Realm
The Ladies' Field
The Sketch
The Strand Magazine
The Harmsworth Monthly Pictorial Magazine

Online
Wikipedia
Manor House - PBS Masterpiece Theater
The History of Hinchingbrooke House
BBC

Fiction
A Room with a View by E. M. Forster
Complete Works of Henry James by Henry James
The Edwardians by Vita Sackville-West
Howards End by E. M. Forster
Night and Day by Virginia Woolf
The Riddle of the Sands by Erskine Childers
The Shuttle by Frances Hodgson Burnett
The Thirty-Nine Steps by John Buchan
The Type-writer Girl by Grant Allen writing as Olive Pratt Rayner
The Visits Of Elizabeth by Elinor Glyn
Works of E. Phillips Oppenheim

ABOUT THE AUTHOR

Evangeline Holland began blogging at Edwardian Promenade to share snippets of information from her research of the Edwardian era, but it has morphed into something amazing and rewarding. She writes romantic historical fiction, and hopes that someday soon, her books will find their way onto the shelves of your local (e-) bookstore. If you have any questions or feedback please email: evangeline@edwardianpromenade.com

Edwardian Promenade
Twitter
Facebook

Other Titles

Pocket Guide to Historical Research

Lady Myddelton's Lover